W9-DDD-783

The Senegalese Novel by Women

Francophone Cultures and Literatures

Tamara Alvarez-Detrell and Michael Paulson
General Editors

Vol. 7

PETER LANG
New York • Washington, D.C./Baltimore • San Francisco
Bern • Frankfurt am Main • Berlin • Vienna • Paris

Susan Stringer

The Senegalese Novel by Women

Through Their Own Eyes

PETER LANG
New York • Washington, D.C./Baltimore • San Francisco
Bern • Frankfurt am Main • Berlin • Vienna • Paris

Library of Congress Cataloging-in-Publication Data

Stringer, Susan.
The Senegalese novel by women:
through their own eyes/ Susan Stringer.
p. cm. — (Francophone cultures and literatures; vol. 7)
Includes bibliographical references and index.
1. Senegalese fiction (French)—Women authors—History and criticism.
2. Women and literature—Senegal—History. I. Series.
PQ3988.5.S38S77   843—dc20   94-34709
ISBN 0-8204-2664-4
ISSN 1077-0186

Die Deutsche Bibliothek-CIP-Einheitsaufnahme

Stringer, Susan:
The Senegalese novel by women:
through their own eyes/ Susan Stringer.—New York;
Washington, D.C./Baltimore; San Francisco; Bern; Frankfurt am Main;
Berlin; Vienna; Paris: Lang.
(Francophone cultures and literatures; Vol. 7)
ISBN 0-8204-2664-4
NE: GT

Cover design by Nona Reuter.

The paper in this book meets the guidelines for permanence and durability
of the Committee on Production Guidelines for Book Longevity
of the Council of Library Resources.

© 1996 Peter Lang Publishing, Inc., New York

Printed in the United States of America.

To my husband, Raimundo.

Contents

I

Introduction

During the 1930s, black students in Paris from the French Caribbean and French West Africa began to think about their specific cultural heritage. In 1932, the journal *Légitime Défense* was published by students from Martinique and, although limited to one issue, this event is often regarded as the official beginnings of black francophone literature. In 1934, a group of Caribbean and African students, including Aimé Césaire, Léon Damas and Léopold Senghor, established another journal, *L'Etudiant noir*. It appeared until publication was halted by World War II. These men were founders of the Negritude movement, an attempt to express and promote the black personality through literature. By its very nature it became a focus for protest against colonialism and political repression. Négritude was primarily associated with poetry, an excellent medium through which to voice revolt, and in 1948 Senghor published his now famous *Anthologie de la nouvelle poésie nègre et malgache de langue française* with the equally famous preface by Jean-Paul Sartre, "Orphée noir."

Although accounts of the beginnings of Black African literature have centered on the Négritude movement, the first African novel was published in 1921 by René Maran, a Guyanese in the French administration in Africa. It was called *Batouala* and it received the Prix Goncourt. Several more novels appeared in the thirties, including *Doguicimi* by the Dahomeyan, Paul Hazoumé, and *Karim* by the

Senegalese, Ousmane Socé. Yet *L'Enfant noir* (1953), by the Guinean
Camara Laye, is the real beginning of the West African novel as an
influential means of literary expression. Despite the frequently
emphasized fact that the novel is an imported western form, its narrative
structure is clearly related to that of oral literature, so that literate
Africans have adopted it with ease. At the same time, the novel is ideally
suited to the presentation and analysis of social reality and social change
in a way that poetry is not. Jacques Chevrier compares the rise of the
novel in eighteenth-century France, in close connection with the
expansion of the bourgeoisie, with its development in Africa at the
moment of significant social change preceding Independence. He sees
both the French and African novels as expressions of the self-
consciousness of a particular social group (98). Sunday Anozie also
relates the evolution of the African novel to the new social and
psychological situation. The flexibility of the novel form allows it to
present what he calls an orchestrated version of the new reality (15).

It was clear by the 1950s that colonialism was a dying force and that
educated Africans were no longer prepared to accept without questioning
the imposition of a foreign culture and political system. Most novels of
this period therefore criticize, either directly or obliquely, the colonial
administration and its ideology, or at least the idea of white supremacy.
As Mohamadou Kane says in "The African Writer and his Public":

> Our writers showed their readiness to become fully engaged–a readiness which
> was to affect the orientation of African literature since the writers wished to avoid
> all gratuitousness in art and were ready to fight colonialism in all its forms until
> it would be wiped out for good as far as their country was concerned (53).

L'Enfant noir was condemned by some Africans for its lack of
"engagement" in the anti-colonial cause. Yet the nostalgia expressed by
Laye for the lost world of his traditional African childhood as he saw it
from France was an illustration of how the French education system
alienated Africans from their own culture. A year later, Laye exposed

more clearly his belief in the spiritual superiority of the Black African world by publishing *Le Regard du roi*. The white protagonist, Clarence, undergoes a positive metamorphosis as he slowly becomes assimilated into African culture while searching for a quasi-mythical African king representing love. Nevertheless, the most virulent attacks on colonialism appeared in the satiric novels of the Cameroonians Mongo Beti and Ferdinand Oyono, while the works of the Senegalese, Sembène Ousmane and Cheikh Hamidou Kane, and of Bernard Dadié from the Ivory Coast all exposed in their own way the problems of colonialism and cultural conflict, of racial oppression and prejudice, and of the loss of traditional African values. Thus, from the beginning, the African novel was seen to have a social role, to be by its very nature "engagé." Although some writers fell silent with the advent of Independence, others have discovered new themes which are equally representative of their attitude of commitment. As Wole Soyinka says in his *Myth, Literature and the African World*: "The writer is far more preoccupied with visionary projection of society than with speculative projections of the nature of literature, or of any other medium of expression" (64).

Women's Writing

There were no women among the pre-Independence African novelists. The first women did not appear until well into the sixties and then only in English-speaking countries. Grace Ogot, Charity Waciuma and Miriam Were, from Kenya, Flora Nwapa of Nigeria and the South African, Bessie Head, all published their first books between 1966 and 1969. In French-speaking Black Africa, women began to write about ten years later and remained largely unknown. Roseann Bell in an article published in 1978 entitled "The Absence of the African Woman Writer" says (incorrectly) that there are no francophone women writers. Sonia Lee makes the same claim in a collection entitled *Sturdy Black Bridges: Visions of Black Women in Literature* which appeared the following year. In 1981, Lloyd Brown maintains in the introduction to his book *Women Writers in Black Africa* that all women writers of any significance write in English and limits his discussion to these women. Yet Patrick Mérand and Séwanou Dabla mention fifteen women novelists and poets in their bibliography of francophone African literature published in 1979 and Brenda Berrian in her *Bibliography of African Women Writers and Journalists* (1985) names more than twice that number, although she points out at the beginning of her book that the overwhelming majority of African women writers communicate in English. In some of her sections, such as those listing short stories, performed plays, conference papers or speeches, broadcast literature and book reviews by francophone writers of books in French, she has no representative from French-speaking Black Africa. She is mistaken about the short stories, however, as Pierre Klein presents two by women in his *Anthologie de la nouvelle sénégalaise (1970–1977)*[1] and two more were published in *Trois Nouvelles*[2] by Les Nouvelles Editions Africaines in 1982. Christine Guyonneau's "Francophone Women Writers from Sub-Saharan Africa: A Preliminary Bibliography," also appearing in 1985, included well over a hundred women from fourteen countries. Finally, in a 1992 article, Jean-Marie Volet talks of a total corpus of about fifty novels written by francophone women from Black Africa.

When one considers that Aoua Keita of Mali won the Grand Prix Littéraire de l'Afrique Noire in 1976 for her autobiographical work, *Femme d'Afrique*, and that Mariama Bâ of Senegal was awarded the first ever Noma Prize for her novel, *Une Si Longue Lettre*, it is surprising that the critical world in general long remained ignorant of the literary output of francophone African women. Oladele Taiwo in his *Female Novelists of Modern Africa* (1984) only discusses women writing in English or translated into English, so that his treatment of francophone writers is limited to two pages on Bâ and a brief mention of her compatriot, Aminata Sow Fall. Jacques Chevrier, in a 1984 revised edition of his *Littérature nègre*, does insert a section entitled "Une écriture féminine", but again, it is only a few pages long. Katherine Frank claims in her article "Feminist Criticism and the African Novel" (1984) that so little work has been done on women writers because the scholars and critics are nearly all men, "who have tended to ignore the admittedly small but still significant number of African women writers and women-related issues in African literature" (35). The Nigerian male critic, Femi Ojo-Ade, agrees with her in his "Female Writers, Male Critics" (1982). He claims: "African literature is a male-created, male oriented, chauvinistic art . . . Male is the master; male constitutes majority—in the sense that they dominate. Women are Disadvantaged, Exploited, Excluded" (158). Coming from the pen of a man so scathing about women's liberation in an article on Bâ's *Une Si Longue Lettre*, this is a surprising statement and one wonders whether he is writing tongue-in-cheek. Yet he appears to be serious and makes the point at the end of this later article that some men believe that the criticism of female literature is a secondary art. In the last few years the situation has changed. There is a marked interest in women writers from francophone Africa, reflected in the increased number of conference papers and journal articles devoted to their works.

Why did women begin writing later than men and why did women in French-speaking countries start almost a decade later than their English-speaking counterparts? A way to approach these questions is to look first at the general status of women in Black African societies. There is considerable disagreement about whether this was increased or decreased by colonialism and related to this is a controversy about whether African women need "liberating" or not. In "Constructive Elements of a Civilization of African Negro Inspiration" (1959) Senghor claims: "Contrary to popular opinion, the Negro-African woman does not need liberation; she has been free for thousands of years" (278). Theresa Ndongko also says the idea African women are oppressed, first by their parents and then by their husbands, does not correspond to reality. She says that women have authority in the home and in their own institutions, that they work in the fields, prepare food, and trade in the markets and that a married woman has a life of her own. She says that in Cameroon there is a fixed division of labor and that women may acquire a degree of economic independence through owning livestock and fields. She does admit, however, that men are in a socially and economically superior position. George Brooks, in his article on women entrepreneurs in eighteenth-century Senegal, affirms that women from the Wolof and Lebou tribes had considerable freedom of action in earlier times and quickly became active in commerce with the Europeans, but that this situation seems to have changed later when the French made Senegal an official colony. Hafkin and Bay, however, claim that most African societies have a strong bias towards male supremacy and that the economic independence so often mentioned by the promulgators of the free African woman is "less a mark of privilege than a matter of necessity" (7). Traditionally, the woman is responsible for feeding and providing for her children, a situation creating hardship for urban women, according to Judith Van Allen, if they do not own land. Others, too, cast doubt on the traditionally free theory. Roseann Bell (1978) calls the assertion that African women have always been liberated "Westerners' trite cliché" (494) and Lloyd Brown claims that inequality was not only brought about by colonialism but also exists today because of "the mores of traditional African society" (5).

Even if one accepts the relative prominence of women in pre-colonial times, there were often what Hafkin and Bay call "culturally legitimated ways to ensure the subordination of women" (9), such as clitoridectomy, menstrual taboos, and the practice of kneeling before men, all of which, they believe, reveal the sexual inferiority of women. In an article on Senegal, Madeleine Deves says, however, that the power of women has declined, but she attributes this to the spread of Islam, since, according to her, Moslems consider that the woman "is an impure being and regarded as a minor" (313). She also mentions the belief that an unmarried woman cannot enter paradise and that a married woman can only do so through the intercession of her husband, stressing that repudiation is an imported Moslem practice.

As for the impact of colonialism, Hafkin and Bay claim in their introduction that research now suggests that it reduced the rights of women because the colonial powers ignored women and dealt only with men, especially with regard to agriculture. Although Sub-Saharan Africa is what Van Allen calls a "female-farming area" (60), the colonizers assumed that men knew more about cultivation than women, because of sex roles in European agriculture. Van Allen says that colonization and modernization "seem to have weakened or destroyed the equality and authority some African women had achieved" (60). Even as late as the seventies, according to her, only men were being trained in new farming techniques and through a combination of male control over land and the prejudices of foreign experts, cash-cropping has become virtually a male monopoly. Although the retail market trade in the towns is dominated by women, the so-called "modern" sector (shops, industries, and offices) is controlled by men, except schools and clinics where educated women work as teachers and nurses. As Van Allen concludes: "Motherhood continues to provide the basic self-identity of African women. In the absence of all or most outside economic, social, and political activities, it has become almost the only identity she has" (64).

Yet it is the sphere of formal education that seems to be crucial with regard to the questions about women writers. Under French rule, very few children, male or female, went to the colonial schools for any length of time. Omar Ka says that education was largely confined to the urban elite and that in 1960 only 10%–25% of children were at school. He reveals that in 1964–1965 only 11% of Senegalese males and 1% of females said that they could read and write French (278). This means that the population as a whole remained illiterate, as West African languages are not traditionally written. Islam had brought Arabic, but despite the widespread existence of Coranic schools, it seems that little was taught in them, if one accepts the testimony of Moussa Ly Sangaré and Amar Samb in their autobiographies. Written Arabic did not become generally known and its use has been largely confined to the religious context. Thus the concept of written language is alien to most West Africans. Even though French continued to be the official language of Senegal after Independence, Carrie Dailey Moore's research shows no improvement over time. She established that even in the 1970s less than twenty percent of the population of Senegal had a reasonable knowledge of French (80). The writers of the Negritude movement and the novelists of the fifties and sixties usually came from a tiny, educationally privileged elite. As Cheikh Hamidou Kane reveals in his celebrated novel *L'Aventure ambiguë*, even when families decided to send their sons to the colonial school, there was on the whole no question of sending daughters, especially in a Moslem country like Senegal. Michael Crowder tells us in *Senegal: A Study in French Assimilation Policy* that in 1938 there were 18,000 boys but only 1,500 girls at school (27) and he also refers to Senegal as a society "where Islam has retarded female education" (68). Aminata Sow and Rose Senghor reveal in an article entitled "Le Rôle d'educatrice de la femme africaine dans la civilisation traditionnelle" that one reason why African societies were so reluctant to send their children to school, especially the girls, was that the colonial school system considerably reduced the role of the family, and particularly of the mother, in the child's upbringing. In traditional society, the main aim of a girl's education was to turn her into a good wife and mother (240). There is an illuminating passage on the mistrust of European education for girls in Malick Dia's autobiographical novel *L'Impossible Compromis*. He explains the mentality of his father's generation. They believed it was sometimes necessary for boys to go to the foreigners' school but girls did not need formal schooling to be good wives. Dia then adds a second and perhaps more important reason. He says his father believed the colonial teaching system destroyed the foundations of African culture, of which women are both the main depositories and the permanent guardians (81). Denise Paulme also talks about the number of girls in school in Africa being greatly inferior to that of boys, referring to the situation at about Independence (21). More than a decade later, Rita Cruise O'Brien says that the standard of education of most Senegalese women was still extremely low and adds that they had an inferior status in general, living in a Moslem society (253). In Paulme's book, Solange Faladé reports on her investigations among women from Greater Dakar during the late fifties. Her subjects were 145 women from the middle class whom she took to be representative of the majority of women there. Some, but very few, had had a French education, but then only for three or four years and none of them continued to use French later. The situation does not seem to have changed radically since that time. Other factors contributing to a lack of interest even now in education for girls are mentioned by Van Allen. First, education is seen as an investment, and it is not considered fruitful to invest in a daughter's education, lost to the family-in-law when the daughter marries. Second, even educated men look for a wife to serve their needs. They prefer a woman with at most a secondary school education, it being widely believed that too much education makes a wife disobedient. Van Allen also reveals that most married women do not work after marriage, as they are expected to devote themselves to the family. Advanced studies for women are therefore considered a waste of time and money, an attitude also common in other parts of the world.

Thus lack of education seems to be a major reason for the rarity of women writers in West Africa. The acquisition of a high level of English or French, the two most common written languages, requires many years of formal learning, as these languages are not normally spoken outside the classroom. Until women began to enter higher education in significant numbers, there was no real possibility of the emergence of a group of women writers.

Education may, however, be only partly responsible for the situation. Patrick Mérand says in *La Vie quotidienne en Afrique noire à travers la littérature africaine d'expression française* that women are born to be silent when men are present or when men are speaking. He refers to a Mandingo myth in which God, wishing to test man and woman, gave each a knife and told each one separately to slit the other's throat. Man, horrified by the idea, chose to disobey, but woman prepared to execute the order. As a punishment, God confined women to the home and the fields under the domination of men. From that day on, women were condemned to keep their opinions to themselves (96). The results of Mérand's research on the feminine condition as seen through literature can be summarized under the headings he gives to the relevant sections of his book: "Née pour travailler" (Born to work), "Née pour procréer" (Born to procreate) and "Née pour se taire" (Born to remain silent). Charlotte Bruner in "Women Writers and Women's Role in Contemporary Black Africa" says that even when women have a profession, they are encouraged to remain inconspicuous, so that social criticism is an unacceptable feminine activity. The novelist, Mariama Bâ, supports this assertion in an article entitled "La Fonction politique des littératures africaines écrites," although she claims that women who protest are marginalized in all cultures. She explains the lack of women writers in Africa as the result of women's reluctance to put down their thoughts in print "pour l'éternité" (6), even though they have plenty to say.

Another Senegalese novelist, Aminata Sow Fall, makes the same point in a 1985 interview with Françoise Pfaff. She says that writing is seen as a form of boldness, shunned by women because they have been taught to be discreet (136). This hesitation on the part of women to express themselves freely is underlined by the results of Awa Thiam's research. She held a collective interview in Guinea with seven men and six women, which she includes verbatim in her book, *La Parole aux Négresses*. In this interview the group was asked about the position of women in society and about the relationship between men and women. All of the men participated, but only two of the women said anything at all, and that very briefly. Although the men were better educated than the women (three had degrees, as opposed to none of the women, although one woman was in the process of acquiring a degree), lack of education did not discourage the men from talking. Rather cultural conditioning seems to have been the determining factor. Maryse Condé, however, feels that neither lack of education nor modesty has kept women silent: "Isn't it rather the very complexity of her condition which forces the African woman to remain silent since she feels unable to come to terms with it?" (133). Whether this is true or not is difficult to establish.

Despite social limitations on the self-expression of women, it should be stressed that their traditional educative role with regard to children is of the utmost importance. It is women who hand down the collective ancestral wisdom to the younger generation, particularly through the art of story-telling. Like many other Africans, Birago Diop in the introduction to his *Les Contes d'Amadou-Koumba* remembers the stories told by his mother and grandmother at the fireside at night and pays homage to the role of women in safeguarding the cultural heritage. One might therefore think that with the advent of the written word, women would take up the same role in literature. Although some women are now writing for children, this is a very recent phenomenon. In the previously mentioned paper, Bruner reveals that although women have always taught children on a daily basis, men traditionally perform prestigious story-telling or epic chant, for a mixed audience and not primarily for children. In addition, *griots* (the African bards, the guardians of history and genealogy) are generally men, not women. Bruner emphasizes that women have always played a very private role in society, confined on the whole to their own family circle. Paulme supports this by claiming that the greatest obstacle to the advancement of women is their distrust first of all of the world outside the home and secondly of their husbands (22). Bruner quotes a United Nations Review (1976−1980) examining the lack of participation of African women in the modernization process, for which it established three reasons: poor education, traditional attitudes about sex roles, and limited credit facilities. The first two reasons confirm what has been said about the lack of women writers, although the third reason would not appear directly relevant to our study. Justice Annie Jiagge, in a paper given in Abidjan in 1972, presents six factors which work against the evolution of women's status. These are a lack of vocational training and of education in general, too many domestic duties and too many children, little interest on the part of women in civic and political responsibility, economic and political dependence on men with an accompanying lack of self-confidence in many areas, and, finally, the existence of polygamy, the dowry system, and customs relating to widowhood. It would seem that most of these factors have contributed to the scarcity of women writers.

Yet the earlier emergence of women writers in English-speaking countries remains unexplained, unless it is related to the situation of women in Moslem countries. Madeleine Deves claims that religious congregations (we presume she means Christian ones, as she has just been severely criticizing Islam) speeded up the entry of girls into schools (325). As countries like Kenya, Ghana and the Ibo region of Nigeria, all of which produced early women writers, were more influenced by Christianity than by Islam, this may be the deciding factor. Yet some of the former French or Belgian colonies, such as the Ivory Coast, Cameroon, Congo, and Zaïre, have very few Moslems and a high percentage of Christians, but they did not produce early women writers. The reason may lie in the differences between the two colonial education systems. In his essay, "The 1914–1918 European war and West Africa" in *History of West Africa*, Michael Crowder says that educational opportunities were far fewer in French territories than in British territories (512). Yet there was a significant number of early male writers from both Christian and Moslem francophone areas. It seems, however, that fewer girls may have attended school in French West Africa. Jarmila Ortova, writing in 1969, explains the total absence of women writers in francophone Africa with the observation that it was very rare for a woman to receive any form of higher education (70). When Pfaff in the afore-mentioned interview asks Aminata Sow Fall why there are more anglophone women writers, Sow Fall is unable to give a precise answer and simply says that perhaps women in Senegal are not particularly interested in literature. She sees no barriers to women becoming writers if they so wish and emphatically disagrees with Pfaff's suggestion that Islam is an important determinant. She mentions the fact that there were very few women writers in France until recent times. The existing ones were exceptional individuals, transcending the norms of their society. Perhaps Sow Fall is right and in a final analysis the discrepancy between the number of African women writing in English and those writing in French cannot simply be explained by religious, social and educational conditions.

Special Position of Senegal

The position of Senegal under French colonial rule in Sub-Saharan Africa was an exceptional one, as Dorothy Blair emphasizes in the introduction to her *Senegalese Literature: A Critical History*. This eminence can be seen in the realm of education. As Crowder says in his book on Senegal: "Until recent years, Senegal was the only territory with an educational system in any way compatible with a policy of assimilation" (5). In 1821, the first government was appointed with the mission of developing the country as a center of French civilization and the first schools were opened the following year. Between 1872 and 1887, the four communes of Gorée, Saint-Louis, Rufisque and Dakar were created. These communes were significant because their residents had a unique right to French citizenship. In 1887, the Ecole Normale William Ponty, which Crowder and O'Brien call "the Eton of West Africa" (674) because many future African leaders were trained there, was founded on the island of Gorée. Following the formation of French West Africa in 1895, Dakar became its official capital in 1902. I.F.A.N. (Institut Français d'Afrique Noire) was established in Dakar in 1938. In 1959, the University of Dakar was formed from the Institut des Hautes Etudes, a joint outpost of the Universities of Paris and Bordeaux. It was called the "eighteenth university of France" and was designed to serve the whole of French West Africa.

The first Black African intellectuals came from Senegal. The most famous, Léopold Senghor, was the first Black African to pass the prestigious competitive examination, the Agrégation, and more recently the first Black African to be elected to the Académie Française (1983). In addition, he was a leader of the Negritude movement and is arguably the most important African poet of the twentieth century. Another Senegalese, Alioune Diop, founded the publishing house and accompanying journal, *Présence Africaine*, both playing an important role in the development of African literature and African studies. An equally significant contribution is being made by Les Nouvelles Editions Africaines, which began publishing in Dakar in 1971 and now has branches in Abidjan and Lomé.

In her preface, Blair says that she used to argue against the existence of national literatures in Africa, but now believes that Senegal is a special case, because since pre-colonial times Senegal has had more natural unity and fewer internal differences based on religious, ethnic and regional considerations than other parts of Black Africa. According to Sheldon Gellar, more than ninety percent of Senegalese are Moslems (88). Although only about one third of the population is ethnically Wolof, the Wolof language is understood by most people, according to Blair (7) and Crowder (77). Wolof, the "national" language of Senegal, is the most important second language for non-Wolofs, not French, the "official" language. This situation is in marked contrast to more linguistically and ethnically varied countries previously under French rule, where French is by necessity the *lingua franca*. Crowder sums up the special situation of Senegal: "Nearly three-quarters of the population have closer historical and ethnic connections than exist in any other area of West Africa save Hausaland in Northern Nigeria" (77). The relatively high rate of urbanization has also contributed to the partial elimination of tribal differences. According to Pierre Fougeyrollas, as early as 1961 twenty-three percent of the population were urbanized, and this percentage has risen steadily.

Fougeyrollas also asserts that Senegal attached more importance to school attendance than any other Black African state. Mérand's 1970s statistics in *La Vie quotidienne en Afrique Noire*, no longer put Senegal in first place, but out of fourteen French-speaking countries, Senegal still had the third highest rate of attendance at institutions of higher education after Congo and Zaïre. Ivory Coast had a population of about nine million, but it had only 6,500 students in higher education compared to Senegal's 7,000, the population of Senegal being only about six million at that time (51).

It is generally recognized that Senegalese novelists have played an exceptionally prominent role in African literature since the fifties. In his 1993 article entitled "Senegalese Literature Today," Laurence Porter points out that "a small population has produced an astonishing amount of first-rate literature"(887). Among the most prominent novelists are Abdoulaye Sadji, Cheikh Hamidou Kane and Sembène Ousmane. Even Bernard Dadié, originally from the Ivory Coast, spent many years in Senegal as a student at the Ecole Normale William Ponty and later as a government official. Although there were no women prose writers in print until the 1970s, the first Black African poetess to publish a collection of poems was the Senegalese, Annette M'Baye, whose *Poèmes africains* appeared in 1965. Senegal is the first predominantly Islamic territory of francophone Black Africa to produce successful women novelists, Mariama Bâ's *Une Si Longue Lettre* being frequently labeled the first truly "feminist" African novel. In Mérand's bibliography, five of the fifteen women writers mentioned (113) are Senegalese, three of them novelists (Bâ, Aminata Sow Fall, Nafissatou Diallo). In Berrian's bibliography, five of the nine novels cited are by Senegalese. Chevrier's new edition briefly discusses eight women writers, three of them the Senegalese novelists mentioned above. Guyonneau's bibliography covers thirty pages, of which eight are devoted to Senegal, by far the greatest number, compared with five to Zaïre, four to Cameroon and one to Ivory Coast. Half the novels she lists are by Senegalese women. Senegal's contribution to Black African literature by both male and female writers is therefore far out of proportion to her population. The literary output of the women alone justifies this study of their work. In general, women writers have preferred the medium of the novel, rather than that of poetry or the theater, a tendency possibly related to the function of the novel as a mirror of social change.

Approach of the Study

A valid approach for the analysis of novels by Senegalese women is the determination of the extent to which the writing reflects their own lives. It is commonly accepted that autobiography occupies a prominent place in Black African writing by men. In his article, "Structures: Sur les 'formes traditionnelles' du roman africain," Mohamadou Kane points out that autobiography is one of the most obvious characterizations of the African novel (561). Chevrier, talking about the situation at Independence, claims that the wave of autobiographical novels was threatening African literature with sclerosis (228). James Olney in his *Tell me Africa: An Approach to African Literature* agrees that African literature is too autobiographical, but finds the genre valuable as an introduction to true fiction. African autobiography being different from its western counterpart because of the relationship between the individual and the group, Olney says that "personal literary expression tends very frequently to shade off into cultural expression" (43). He feels that the prominence of this form is indicative of the role the African novelist has assigned himself, that of the exponent of African culture. Kane supports this view. He says that African novelists bear witness to their own society from a personal standpoint (561). Dan Izevbaye makes a similar statement in that he claims that autobiography is so important in Africa because it satisfies the creative urge and yet is socially relevant. In his opinion, because the African novelist sees himself as a cultural model and is almost without exception committed to a social or political role, autobiography is a way of affirming emotional involvement in a way impossible in historical or sociological writing. Georges May, although referring to European writing, points out that autobiography is perhaps the literary form that most unites the writer and the reader (111). He says that the reader has a natural tendency to relate his own life to that of the autobiographer, even if only through the emotions expressed. Yet for Kane, the autobiography is a primary stage in the development of the novel and he claims that a novelist who has reached maturity in his art distances himself from his subject. Robert Pageard calls "le roman à tendance autobiographique" the simplest form in his classification of African novels (64). Olney implies, too, that novelists often begin with autobiography and move away from it in subsequent writing.

When Olney was working on his book in the early seventies, there was virtually nothing written by women from Black Africa that could be classified as autobiographical and the little there was had been published in English. The situation is different now. Guyonneau mentions eight autobiographies from francophone West Africa alone as compared with twenty novels. Régina Lambrech emphasizes the importance of the form in an article entitled "Three Black Women, Three Autobiographers" (1982). She states: "Since it is about one's own experiences that one is most knowledgeable and perhaps, also, most eloquent, it is therefore logical that the literary genre most chosen by contemporary Black African women writers is autobiography" (136). Apart from my disagreement with her categorization of *La Brise du Jour* by the Cameroonian, Lydie Dooh-Bunya, as an autobiography, I would also like to point out that Lambrech was writing at a time when very little had been published by women. Nevertheless, her claim about the preeminence of the autobiographical form should be examined and tested in this study.

Lambrech says that it is up to black women to tell the truth about themselves and sees their role as writers as that of illuminators of the female condition. Whether African women writers themselves have the same view of their role is the basic consideration underlying my study. This is the fundamental question to be asked about women's literature at this stage in its development. That is, I intend to examine women's writing from the gender perspective. Assuming that these women, like their male counterparts, see themselves as teacher-educators, and that therefore women's writing reflects and comments on the changing social reality, what image of women do they present? This approach involves, as the other dimension of the same problematic, an analysis of the male condition as seen by women writers. It may be that some of the writers under discussion attempt to avoid a strictly feminine perspective and rather set out to analyze social problems in general. It may be that they are more interested in individuals than types or models. Within the above context, it will be necessary to establish the place of the autobiographical form, to see if it really plays such a significant role in female writing.

Other relevant questions are the following: Do the women writers under consideration pass through a primary autobiographical stage and then turn to more universal themes? How are their themes related to those in male writing? For whom are these women writing? Such considerations do not exclude an investigation into the literary value of the texts. In good literature, form and content create a harmonious whole. Yet my primary concern is with content, with the world as seen through the eyes of some Senegalese women who decided to speak.

II

Nafissatou Diallo

The first recorded Senegalese woman prose writer is Nafissatou Diallo. Born 1941, she published *De Tilène au Plateau* in 1975. Like the Malian, Aoua Keita, whose book *Femme d'Afrique* appeared in the same year, she chose to write an autobiography. Diallo's second book, *Le Fort maudit*, a historical novel, came out five years later in 1980, followed by *Awa la petite marchande* in 1981, the year of her death. Her final novel, *La Princesse de Tiali*, was published posthumously in 1987.[3]

As already indicated, it took some time for the earliest works by women to reach the world at large and nobody seems to have commented on them until the 1980s. Of Diallo's four books, her autobiography has aroused the most interest, being hailed as the birth of Senegalese feminine literature. Charlotte Bruner, in a 1983 review of the English translation, calls *De Tilène au Plateau*, "a real first" and "a woman's voice so long awaited." She writes: "Nafissatou Diallo has broken through the wall of silence which until very recently inhibited the literary expression of Francophone African women" (339). Yet the commentators focus on the content, rather than the literary achievement. Pramila Bennett, again referring to the English translation, feels that such books "provide a real link between cultures–everyone, vividly aware of their own upbringing, can relate to the intense emotions as well as the obvious differences" (71). In her opinion, the very ordinariness of the life depicted makes *De Tilène au Plateau* important. Blair also stresses the cross-cultural aspect: "The essence of the book's appeal, which to my mind will make it a minor classic, is the universality of Safi's story with which girls of all cultures and backgrounds can identify" (120).

In a book review, Emile Langlois very briefly compares the role of *De Tilène au Plateau* to that of Camara Laye's *L'Enfant noir* (169). To illuminate Diallo's purpose in writing her first work and to place it in the context of women's writing, I would like to elaborate on that comparison by relating her reasons to those of Laye, whose autobiographical narrative is considered to mark the beginning of the West African novel as a literary corpus. In a paper entitled "The soul of Africa in Guinea," Laye explains how he came to write *L'Enfant noir*. A student in Paris feeling cold and lonely, he began to evoke for himself the warmth of his native Africa and the love imbuing his childhood and adolescence. Jotting down his memories for his own pleasure, he was later persuaded by a friend to edit the notes and offer them to a publisher, who accepted the manuscript. Although Laye's work is a highly personalized account of his early life, he was also conscious of its historical aspect. In his paper he says: "I was drawing a picture of my native Guinea which was certainly quite unlike the picture she would be presenting to the world within a few years and different, too, from the one she was presenting already" (67).

In the preface to *De Tilène au Plateau*, Diallo explains how and why she wrote her autobiography:

Je ne suis pas une héroïne de roman mais une femme toute simple de ce pays: une mère de famille et une professionnelle (sage-femme et puériculturiste) à qui sa maison et son métier laissent peu de loisir.

A la clinique toutefois, en dehors des heures d'activités intenses du matin consacrées aux enfants malades, la consultation des enfants sains l'après-midi laisse des moments flottants que le personnel consacre à la lecture, à la couture, au tricotage.

Depuis quelques semaines, je me suis mise à écrire. Sur quoi écrirait une femme qui ne prétend ni à une imagination débordante ni à un talent d'écrire singulier? Sur elle-même, bien sûr. Voici donc mon enfance et ma jeunesse telles

que je me les rappelle. Le Sénégal a changé en une génération. Peut-être valait-il
la peine de rappeler aux nouvelles pousses ce que nous fûmes.

I am not the heroine of a novel but an ordinary woman of this country, Senegal:
a mother and a working woman–a midwife and child-welfare nurse–whose home
and career leave her very little free time.

However, at the Maternity and Child Welfare Centre in Ouagou-Niane where
I work, although the mornings are very busy seeing sick children, during the
afternoons when we see healthy children there are some gaps between
consultations which the staff spend in reading sewing or knitting.

For the last few weeks I have started to write. What would a woman write
about who has no claim to any exceptional imagination or outstanding literary
talent? She could only write about herself, of course. So here are my memories
of my childhood and adolescence. Senegal has changed in a generation. Perhaps
it is worth reminding today's youngsters what we were like when we were their
age.[4]

The parallels between the two authors are striking. Like that of Laye,
Diallo's vocation began in a casual manner in her spare time, and it is
also possible that her manuscript arrived at publication in a similar way.
Although she is writing twenty years after him, her childhood also
belongs to a disappearing world she is anxious to describe to her younger
compatriots. That both writers see themselves as representative cases is
clear from the titles of their works: the young Camara Laye is "l'enfant
noir" (the black child) while Diallo's early life as expressed in the subtitle of *De Tilène au Plateau* becomes "une enfance dakaroise" (a Dakar
childhood.) To underline her representative role, Diallo claims from the
outset that she is an ordinary Senegalese woman, not the heroine of a
novel. Laye gave his paper ten years after the publication of his first
book, when he was already an established writer. He therefore had no
need to defend his literary talents. In contrast, Diallo feels obliged to
anticipate criticism of her abilities by saying that she has none in
particular. The existence of a preface, as well as its semi-apologetic tone,
could also be related to the public diffidence of African women and to

Diallo's position as first female prose writer.

Within the text proper, Diallo discloses other reasons for writing, springing from her family relationships. In the first chapter she tells us that she serves as the collective memory for her extended family. More importantly, on the very last page she says that her profound grief at her father's death was attenuated by the idea of writing about him:

> Alors je me dis qu'un jour, je parlerais de lui. Il n'avait été ni politicien ni khalife, seulement un homme intègre qui avait vécu jour après jour, comme on exécute un sacerdoce, pour les siens, pour les autres, jamais pour lui, pour les autres, finalement pour ce pays. Je le dirais, à ses enfants, à ses petits-enfants; pourquoi pas au monde? Pourquoi ne pas dire au monde qui vit les yeux braqués sur les grands, que les petits et les modestes sont ceux qui font, soutiennent, et portent les grands? Un juste a vécu; il fut modeste et grand.
>
> Ecrire? Moi? J'entends les ricanements: 'Ecrire un livre pour dire qu'on a aimé Père et Grand-Mère? La belle nouvelle!' J'espère avoir fait un peu plus: avoir été au-delà des tabous de silence qui règnent sur nos émotions (132).

> And so I thought that one day I would write about him. He had been neither a politician nor a caliph, only a man of honour who had lived day after day, as one carries out a holy duty, for his family, for others, and when all's said and done, for this country. I would tell this to his children, to his grandchildren; why should I not tell it to the world? Why should I not say to the world which lives with its eyes fixed on great men and women, that it is the unimportant, modest folk who support and carry the weight of the great? A just man has lived his life; he was modest and great.
>
> Write a book? Me? I can hear you tittering: "Write a book to say that you've loved your father and your grandmother? What's so new about that?" I hope that I have done a little more than that; perhaps I have lifted the taboos of silence that reign over our emotions (133).

Diallo wishes to relive the love she experienced in her relationships with her father and grandmother and to pay tribute to them in her autobiography. There is also the suggestion that the biographies of supposedly ordinary people can be more edifying than those of the famous, and it is clear that her father and grandmother are meant to serve as cultural models, as well as herself. This overt reference to others may once again reflect a desire to reduce the impression of egoism implicit in the autobiographical form. Yet Laye's father and mother also play a central role in his narrative and the prominence of love as a theme establishes another link between the two writers.

Diallo's final reason for writing is one not given explicitly by Laye, although his text reveals its existence. At the end of the passage cited, she refers to the African taboo on the expression of emotions. Her comment illustrates how the intimate nature of autobiography departs from the anonymity of oral literature, which emphasizes the external and the collective even when describing the exploits and virtues of great individuals. At an earlier point in her narrative Diallo explains that Africans are reluctant to display their feelings for fear of being considered both bad-mannered and westernized (ch. 15). Her autobiography is a demonstration of revolt against this taboo.

Thus, despite the difference in time between the publication of their first works, Laye and Diallo essentially share the same purpose. In speaking out for her own gender, Diallo had to begin again where Laye had begun two decades before. She did for African women in 1975 what he had done for men in 1953. The reasons Diallo gives for writing are also closely related to the function of African autobiography in general as established by Olney: the desire to preserve a disappearing world, to describe the African milieu to outsiders and to offer a representative case of a peculiarly African experience (27).

Four Works, Three Sub-genres

Diallo's works all center on a female character, but, superficially at least, they belong to three different sub-genres: autobiography, historical novels, and children's literature. Both Philippe Lejeune (26) and Georges May (179) are convinced there is no essential difference between a novel and an autobiography, except in the attitude of the reader, who believes the autobiographer to exist and to be faithfully recounting his or her life. Diallo presents *De Tilène au Plateau* as her childhood and youth as she remembers them, that is, as a true autobiography, and the reader has no reason to question this assertion. Yet the book has a number of formal characteristics relating it to fiction and to Diallo's later work as a novelist. She does not recount her life in strict chronological order. The lack of concern with precise time is illustrated by the reference to only five dates in the whole text, those which mark the major events of her early life: her birth, her entry into school, the break-up of the extended family, her father's pilgrimage to Mecca, and her father's death. The work also has artistic unity. It closes with the departure of Safi (as Diallo is called in the book) for France and with the death of her father and the impending death of her grandmother. The demise of the old family coincides with the beginning of the new one Safi and her husband will create with the expected birth of their first child in France. Place names are precise and there are sometimes comparisons between present-day Dakar and that of Diallo's childhood, so there is no attempt to avoid the concrete, but in general the episodes are impressionistic and are evidently intended to convey the main relationships in her life and the kind of person she was, as well as the atmosphere and customs of the times, rather than relate a series of facts in the nature of a historical document. This personal quality is the book's strong point and one of the basic attractions of the autobiographical form. The reader identifies simultaneously with the child and with the woman as she looks back on her life, sometimes with joy, sometimes with sorrow. As George May points out, memories of childhood and youth are privileged, as they describe the most universal side of life (107).

As is often the case in an autobiography, there is a constant interplay between past and present. A frequent technique used by Diallo is to recount an episode in the past and then to add one sentence at the very end which brings us into the present. Chapter 23 describes a battle between two gangs of teenage girls, and concludes with the comment that those "Valkyries" are now peace-loving mothers who come to consult her at the clinic. Chapter 27, in which she meets her future husband, falls in love and finally brings her father to accept the marriage, closes with this sentence: "Que de tourments ai-je causés aux miens. Mes enfants m'en causeront-ils autant? Aujourd'hui, c'est avec le sourire que j'écris mon passé. Je tremble encore pour mon bonheur car sans mon audace, il me passait entre les doigts" (112). [What torments I have caused my family! Will my children cause me as many? Today I can smile as I write about my past. I still tremble for my happiness because, if I had been less bold, it would have slipped through my fingers (112).] Not only does Diallo return to the present, but her thoughts move into the future and the life of the next generation.

One aspect of *De Tilène au Plateau* which is sometimes inexplicable is the way in which Diallo uses initials for names. In some cases initials represent a desire for discretion, as with Diallo's first boyfriend, or her husband. But why, when she normally mentions her sisters and aunts by name, does she suddenly talk of "ma soeur D." and "tante F." at the end of chapter 23 and why is her sister referred to as "F" on one page in chapter 24 and as "Fatou" on the following page? This arbitrary use of initials seems to indicate Diallo's ambivalence about revealing the identity of others. She calls her first teacher "Madame Ndèye" and then tells us in a footnote that some proper names have been changed, when the use of an initial would have created anonymity. Perhaps this vacillation is once more related to Diallo's lack of precedent and her natural discretion as an African woman.

Another element which relates the work to fiction rather than to western autobiography is the use of reconstituted speech. The father's words to the family before he leaves for Mecca are put in quotation marks as though Diallo had recorded them and then reproduced them verbatim, which seems highly improbable. The same is done with her boyfriend's love-letter and with her father's advice before her marriage. This device may reflect what Olney calls the African disregard for the facts in the strict western sense (75). What seems to matter is the dramatic effect, communicated in a more immediate way through direct speech.

De Tilène au Plateau targets both a Senegalese and foreign readership. Wolof words are occasionally used, sometimes with explanatory footnotes, sometimes without, when the meaning is obvious. They generally appear where there is no French equivalent: in relation to circumcision rites, to exorcism ceremonies, to the practices associated with the return from Mecca, to African hairstyles. The manner of describing customs or traditions also reveals that Diallo is writing about them with foreigners in mind. At a wedding Safi shows surprise that the gifts for the bride are divided among family members. This distribution is normal, so that Diallo would appear to be anticipating the reactions of her foreign readers. The same can be said when Diallo describes some aspects of Islam, such as the main feasts in the religious calendar, or the importance to Muslims of the pilgrimage to Mecca. Any Senegalese, even a non-Moslem, would know these facts.

Diallo's second and fourth books, *Le Fort maudit* (1980) and the posthumous *La Princesse de Tiali* (1987) are historical novels written in the third person. Although Paul Hazoumé's *Doguicimi* (1938) is the first African historical novel with a woman in the main role, his heroine is a devoted wife who finally buries herself alive in the tomb of her dead husband. Diallo's two works are the first historical narratives with a woman as protagonist in her own right and not merely in her relationship with a man, Africans are deeply conscious of the part played by kings and warriors in their past. History in Africa is basically an account of the lives of such heroes, prominent figures in oral literature. They have largely inspired drama in modern literature, although Mamadou Seyni Mbengue published a novel, *Le Royaume de sable* (1975) about Cayor after the defeat by the French of its most famous leader, Lat Dior.

Le Fort maudit is original because it is an epic novel about a woman. It focuses on the life of the heroine, Thiane Sakher Fall, but also provides us with a picture of life in the Wolof kingdoms of Cayor and Baol before they were colonized and became part of what is now called Senegal. The only date given is that of the founding of the heroine's village by her great-grandfather in 1801. As Cayor was first annexed by the French in 1865, the action evidently takes place before this period.

The book   describes how the leader of Baol, Fariba Nael Ndiaye, invaded and defeated Cayor whose *damel,* or king, is named as Falli Yoro Fall. Virtue rules in Islamic Cayor, but licentiousness is the norm in pagan Baol. Diallo's historical sources are unclear, however. In an article entitled "The Wolof Kingdom of Kayor," Vincent Monteil gives a list (263–264) of the *damels* of Cayor, but there is no mention of Falli Yoro Fall. Nor are the two rulers of Baol mentioned by Diallo in any of the lists discovered by Martin and Becker and published in "Les *Teen* du Baol: Essai de chronologie" (1976). In *Le Fort maudit,* Baol's leaders are presented negatively: Fariba is cruel and his father, the old Bouna Nael Ndiaye, a drunkard. Interestingly, this seems a more appropriate description of the *damels* of Cayor. Monteil says that Birahima Fal (1855–1859) died of "excessive intemperance" (264) and both he and another historian, John Trimingham (177) describe another *damel,* Ma-Kodu, as a drunkard and oppressor of his people. Monteil claims, too, in an article in I. M. Lewis's *Islam in Tropical Africa* that the *damels* of Cayor were consistently opposed to Islam by the beginning of the nineteenth century (167) and that the Cayorian people as a whole were not converted until Lat Dior became a Muslim in 1864 (170). Donal Cruise O'Brien takes issue with Monteil over this matter, however, claiming: "The extent of Islamic diffusion among the Wolof prior to the French conquest of the late nineteenth century has been the subject of widely diverging assessments" (20). He asserts that there was a powerful Islamic faction in Cayor as early as the seventeenth century and that religious change was slower in Baol (21). It is therefore not clear from the historical sources whether Diallo's re-creation of Islamic Cayor is accurate or not. As far as the relationship between Cayor and Baol is concerned, however, there seems to be no doubt that the ruler of Cayor normally established his authority over Baol, rather than the reverse. Cruise O'Brien says that Baol became dependent on Cayor in 1786 when its king died without direct descendants (16). In "The Wolof Kingdom of Cayor," Monteil mentions that the *damel* of Cayor ruled Baol until 1855. There followed, however, a period of fighting which lasted until

1859. It may be that the action in *Le Fort maudit* takes place in this unsettled time. Yet Baol's independence did not last and Monteil says that Lat Dior followed the example of his predecessors in bringing Baol under his rule in 1874 (272). Eunice Charles also stresses the dominating influence of Cayor, saying that it was the strongest Wolof state in the nineteenth century and normally controlled Baol and sometimes another kingdom, Jolof (16). She also states that Cayor maintained its superiority by trading for firearms with the French, a role attributed to Baol in Diallo's novel. Yet Diallo may have had access to other historical sources, leading to her positive depiction of peace-loving, Islamic Cayor in contrast with the degradation of life in pagan Baol. It is also possible that she has to some extent created her own history and historical figures to support the view of an idyllic traditional existence guided by Islam, destroyed first by neighboring pagans and later, by implication, by the French. As for the heroine of the novel, Thiane Sakher Fall, she appears to be fictitious.

Le Fort maudit is not only a historical novel. As André-Patrick Sahel says, the work is meant to be seen from a double perspective: as an account of nineteenth-century customs before the arrival of the Europeans and as a tragic drama. The novel is both the story of the heroine, Thiane Sakher Fall, and that of a people, or strictly speaking of two peoples, although the Baol-Baol are not treated in the same detail as the Cayorians. Neither of these themes is autobiographical in the narrow sense, but both relate to the wider definition of autobiography as established by Olney. Senegalese Muslims of today are meant to identify with their roots in traditional Cayorian life. As for Thiane, although a fictional character, she is put forward as an example of traditional African womanhood, an epic figure to be admired and imitated in her virtues in the same way as the real kings and warriors in oral literature. For this reason, no doubt, Diallo dedicated the novel to her daughters and all the mothers of eternal Africa. At the same time, the occasional aside to explain a practice belonging to Islam or an object unfamiliar to Westerners reveals that Diallo always has non-Senegalese in mind when she is writing, although, in contrast to *De Tilène au Plateau*, very little Wolof is used.

As part of the attempt to create an epic tragedy, the language is much more poetic than that of the first book, as can be seen in the prologue, recounting the moment of Thiane's death. Thus the reader knows the destiny of the heroine before the novel begins:

> Son visage émergeait de l'obscurité et paraissait à la lueur des étoiles comme un masque tragique de souffrance et de haine . . . belle dans sa déchéance, telle apparaissait Thiane Sakher Fall, l'esclave dont le destin, en une nuit, avait fait une martyre (8).

> Her face emerging from the darkness seemed in the light of the stars a tragic mask of suffering and hate . . . beautiful in her decline, thus appeared Thiane Sakher Fall, the slave made martyr by destiny in one night.[5]

Before she dies, Thiane returns in her memory to her happy village childhood, giving the novel a circular structure.

La Princesse de Tiali is also a depiction of life in pre-colonial Senegal. This time, however, there are no dates and no mention of Europeans. The heroine, Fary, grows up in a Muslim village (Mboupène), not geographically situated, although said to be under the suzerainty of the pagan Prince of Tiali, Bocar Djiwan Malick, grandson of Ndiamal Djiwan. Mboupène was founded by Fary's great-grandfather, a *griot* (praise-singer) from the court of the *damel*, so presumably from Cayor, although it is never mentioned by name. The historical context appears to be deliberately vague, because the purpose of this novel goes beyond the re-creation of traditional life and the promotion of Islam to a critique of certain practices and beliefs that have survived into modern times. This view is expressed in the preface by Amadou Samb, referring to outmoded prejudices and taboos he sees as obstacles to the development of Senegal. Thus *La Princesse de Tiali* can be seen as a pseudo-historical novel, despite its descriptions of traditional life.

Like *Le Fort maudit,* it is an account of personal tragedy. The heroine does not die, but she sacrifices her happiness for the good of Islam and of her people. The frequent use of Wolof throughout the text (sometimes with a translation, sometimes without) gives the novel a stronger African flavor than Diallo's previous writings. Much of the narrative is in the form of dialogues in simple informal French, making the text more accessible to a wider public. In this last work, Diallo appears more interested in communicating with her compatriots than anyone else, although the inclusion of cultural explanations, such as that of the Wolof caste system, reveals her persistent awareness of a foreign readership.

The last work published in Diallo's lifetime, *Awa la petite marchande*, is a novel for children from age eleven onward. Because of the importance of literature for the young, especially in Africa where it sometimes replaces traditional stories and legends as a source of moral instruction, it needs to be examined in this study. In form it is what Bede Ssensalo calls a "pseudo-autobiography." Although fiction, it appears to be autobiography. Early in the text the following comment appears: "Je garde encore en moi des souvenirs amers . . . " (13) [I still have bitter memories . . .[6]] so that the reader thinks of Awa as existing and reflecting on her past in the same way that the mature Diallo looks back on her childhood in *De Tilène au Plateau*. Yet this is an isolated remark and the rest of the book is written in the past. Presumably Diallo chose this pseudo-autobiographical form to make her readers identify more closely with the main character.

The book is ostensibly written for children. The style is appropriately simple and there is an explanation of difficult vocabulary at the end. Because of the level of formal education in Africa and the problems with French, it may also be of interest to a section of the adult population, keen to read French but without the knowledge to approach more stylistically sophisticated literature. Like the previous works, this book is aimed at both an indigenous and foreign readership. Certain descriptions, such as the touristic references to Paris or the allusions to the Riviera, are clearly for Africans and others, such as the geographical location of Rufisque or the description of a fisherman's net, for foreigners. Wolof vocabulary is used but is always translated.

Similarities in Form and Content

Although Diallo's works belong to different sub-genres, there are similarities between them in form and content that originate in her own life, as well as in her purpose with regard to women and Senegalese society in general. She has a propensity for a two-part antithetical structure, expressed in her autobiography in the title. Until eleven years old, Safi lives with her extended family in a huge house in the African part of Dakar but separated by a wall and garden from the crowded poverty outside. Her family is privileged and her early life described in idyllic terms. This paradise is destroyed when the family is forced to divide and move to less spacious quarters. It is a sad experience, but not a traumatic one, and Safi quickly accustoms herself to life on the Plateau with new friends. The title of the book is misleading as "De Tilène au Plateau" implies to a Senegalese readership that the family advances socially by moving to the Plateau, the European quarter. In the light of the text, however, it is a mistake to place too much emphasis on duality. The event is important for Safi, but no harsh contrast is presented and her life continues on its pleasant way, despite the change. Yet the move does coincide with her emergence from childhood. She begins to create her own life with her friends and to reduce her dependence on home and family. In this sense, the two periods of Safi's early life find expression in the title of the work.

The duality of structure and content is far more significant in *Le Fort maudit* and is designed to raise the status of the heroine to that of an epic, tragic figure. Initially, there is the strong contrast between the two kingdoms. The first half of the novel presents life in Cayor, a "paradis terrestre" (31) of purity and innocence. Then a short section on neighboring Baol establishes it as the antithesis. Its pagan inhabitants are depraved by sexual orgies and habitual drunkenness and their culture corrupted by contact with European traders.

While the two kingdoms respectively epitomize purity and decadence, their main representatives, the protagonists of the novel, represent good and evil. Thiane is the tragic heroine who sacrifices her life for her people. Fariba is the wicked genius whose ambition and lust for power destroy his feelings for others. Both are portrayed as exceptional beings, whose birth is portentous. Both are associated with supernatural forces through dreams or visions. Both are extraordinarily beautiful. Yet, even as children the joy and virtue of Thiane contrasts with the loneliness and sadism of Fariba.

As Thiane is the incarnation of all that is positive in Cayor, its overthrow and destruction signify the end of her charmed existence in the security of the family. If the first part of the book is a hymn to life, the second is haunted by cruelty and death. The heaven of the village becomes the hell of the Evil Fort, foreseen by Thiane in a dream and by her father in a vision. The defeat of Cayor by warriors from Baol is portrayed as the end of the world in religious terms. The enemy are described as the horsemen of the Apocalypse, spreading Hell in their path. The situation is compared to that of Mohammed in the most difficult battles of his holy war. The survivors, including Thiane, are taken on a nightmarish march to the Evil Fort: "Forteresse impénétrable, entourée d'arbres géants, de soldats hors du temps, presque irréels, dans ce décor de l'aube des temps" (102). [Impenetrable fortress, surrounded by giant trees, by soldiers outside time, almost unreal, in this setting from the beginning of time.]

The contrast between Thiane's life in the village and that at the fort are reflected in the metamorphosis that takes place within the heroine herself. The hardships of captivity bring out her strength and goodness, but the innocent, happy girl no longer exists. She is now driven by hate, particularly for the man who both killed her fiancé and raped and murdered her mother. Even her religious faith has been destroyed. In an episode reminiscent of the Biblical account of the death of Holofernes at the hand of Judith, Thiane seduces her enemy and then assassinates him with a poisoned stick. At the climax of the novel Fariba comes to inspect the fort and Thiane kills him in the same way. This deed is the catharsis in tragic terms: "Thiane était au sommet de l'extase. Elle éprouva une sensation de bien-être, une paix immense comme si son corps, son coeur, son être tout entier étaient à jamais débarrassés du poids de toutes les souffrances de son existence" (125). [Thiane was at the height of ecstasy. She experienced a feeling of well-being, an immense peace as if her body, her heart, her whole self were for ever rid of the weight of all the suffering of her existence.] She then kills herself and the book ends with a poetic lament.

Diallo thus attempts to create an epic tragedy through the contrast between the two parts of *Le Fort maudit*. Whether it really succeeds is a matter of opinion. Sahel obviously feels that it does. The tone is uneven, however, and at times the grandiose style is somewhat strained. Furthermore, there is a conflict between the role of Thiane as a tragic figure in principle embodying forces greater than herself and the highly personal motives and emotions that inspire her revenge.

La Princesse de Tiali also has a bi-partite structure. During the first half of the novel, the heroine Fary lives in the village of Mboupène, but its wretchedness contrasts sharply with Thiane's paradise on earth. The very first chapter emphasizes the bed-bugs, the foul odors, the lack of privacy, the rats, and the rags. As Fary observes the sufferings of her mother in the struggle against poverty, her mind is filled with hate and bitterness and shame. The situation changes after she accompanies her father to the court at Tiali. The prince is bewitched by her beauty and finally makes her his fourth wife in spite of her inferior caste. The second half of the book depicts her life and role as princess, but this is not a fairy-story. The prince is physically repellent and Fary never ceases to hate him. She had given up the man she loved because she believed that as princess she would be able to help her people both spiritually and materially. She sacrifices her own happiness for the cause of Islam (she converts the prince) and to combat the evils of the caste system, particularly to help her own caste, the *griots*. The last page presents the unhappy but stoic figure of Fary at her mother's funeral, thinking of her future with the prince: "Elle le pressera comme un citron, elle le videra jusqu'à la dernière goutte pour la réhabilitation de sa race"(191). [She would squeeze him like a lemon. She would take everything from him to rehabilitate her people (106).[7]]

Awa la petite marchande is also divided into two distinct parts, according to the fortunes of the main character and her family. This duality illustrates Diallo's didactic aims. The first two-thirds of the novel are set in Senegal and the last third in France, where Awa and her father spend three years before returning home at the end. Once again the two sections stand in sharp contrast to each other. Awa, born about 1950 and nine years old at the beginning of the novel, comes from a poor family of fishermen in Rufisque, near Dakar. Her father, Salif, left the sea after his father and brothers were drowned and is now cook and general servant for a rich Lebanese shopkeeper. Her mother, Yacine, is a fish seller. The extended family live together in a compound, but Awa's family is the poorest and because of Salif's work their status is lower.

After a period of misfortune when Salif falls gravely ill and cannot work and Awa is forced to leave school to earn her living as a fish seller, the two of them are offered a position as servants to the Governor returning home. Awa's first impressions of Europe are the usual stereotypical negative ones found in many African works, associated with a lack of physical and human warmth. Yet for them France is the land of opportunity. Salif is transformed, learning to read and write and qualifying as a motor mechanic. Awa finishes her elementary education and obtains her "certificat d'études." Self-confident and optimistic, they return home to a new villa and a comfortable life. The fairy story closes with the following refection: "Une année de peine à présent noyée dans une mer de paix, d'espoir, de richesse et de bonheur" (136) [A year of pain now drowned in a sea of peace, hope, riches, and happiness.]

The similarities between Diallo's four works are not limited to the structure. The reader is also intrigued by the resemblance between the heroines' characters and personal situations, especially their family relationships. Except in the case of Fary, Diallo concentrates on the childhood and youth of her protagonists and their life before marriage.

She does not deal with them as mature adults. Nor are any of them presented in their professional capacity. Diallo describes herself in the preface to *De Tilène au Plateau* as a mother and professional but this dual role is not shown in the autobiography. The work opens when Safi is seven and although it closes with her marriage, studies, and departure for France with her husband, the final events are treated summarily. Nor are the other heroines confronted with problems that older women face. Even Fary, married with several children, is still very young at the end of the novel. Diallo's focus on the youth of her protagonists makes choice a central theme in all the works.

The four girls are strikingly similar in personality and character. All are extraordinarily independent and, except for Awa, somewhat rebellious. Safi, Thiane, and Fary are extroverts and tomboys, always leading their friends into mischief. Awa is just as strongwilled and decided, but is too busy studying and working to indulge in pranks. The girls are not always presented positively, however. They are intolerant and sarcastic towards those more timid than themselves. Safi, or at least the mature Diallo, recognizes her own failings. In *De Tilène au Plateau* she writes of her difficult character and proud nature. Both Safi and Thiane are socially privileged and idyllically happy in childhood, while Awa and Fary are poor and despised. Yet all four heroines are proud and ambitious, representing no doubt Diallo's ideal of what a girl should be.

The family relationships in the three works also resemble each other and are presented as the key to the heroines' success. Safi hero-worships her father, while her grandmother, Mame, is her friend and confidant in place of her dead mother. Mame is also a model and Safi describes her as one of the most complete beings she has ever known (15). Because she has a special place in her grandmother's affections, Safi is allowed freedoms denied to the other girls of the family. Despite her largely traditional attitudes, Mame supports Safi's desire to attend school and encourages her granddaughter's individuality and resourcefulness.

Thiane's family relationships are very similar. Her mother, Ngone, was chosen for her father, Ibra, at birth and married to him at the age of fourteen. Introverted and outwardly submissive during the day, she becomes a passionate lover at night. Although the first of three wives, Ngone is the favorite and an important influence on her husband. To Thiane she is more like a friend than a mother. At the same time, Thiane is her father's favorite child, referred to as his lucky charm and his principal concern. Ibra is a figure of stern authority in his public life, but in his relationship with Thiane and Ngone he is gentle and affectionate. Like Safi's father, he becomes more pious and ascetic as he grows older.

Awa is also very close to her parents, but the relationship is sometimes more problematic because of the social and financial pressures on the family. Her mother, Yacine, is despised and resented by the family-in-law, partly because her maternal grandmother came from another tribe, but also because of her natural dignity and beauty. Her cleanliness is constantly underlined, and one wonders if this is propaganda on the part of Diallo the nurse. Her physical attributes are also described as though they reflect her moral superiority. Yacine is like the stereotype of the mother found throughout African literature: honorable, dignified, hard-working, strict, yet full of love for her husband and children. The father's work, however, is constantly referred to as a source of shame, not only to the extended family but also to Awa. Yet he is also depicted as a figure of authority and an exemplary father and husband, a model of dignity and savoir-faire when he leaves the degrading environment of the Lebanese household. Once again, the relationship of the heroine to her parents is shown to be one of deep mutual respect and love.

Only in *La Princesse de Tiali* is there a deviation from this harmonious image of family life. Fary and her mother, Lala, have the same relationship of love and dependence depicted in the other three works, but her father, Mayacine, is a negative figure in the first part of the novel. He is tyrannical, promiscuous, and brutal. Although she cannot openly rebel against his authority, Fary bitterly resents his humiliating treatment of her mother, especially when he repudiates his fourth wife and marries a sixteen-year-old niece adopted by Lala. Diallo is clearly using Mayacine as a vehicle for social criticism, but after the first fifty pages she is unable to sustain this negativity. During the journey to the court Mayacine becomes the same strong but loving object of respect as the other fathers. For the rest of the novel he is an ideal husband to Lala and there is no further mention of polygamy. This metamorphosis may be attributed to Diallo's relationship with her own father. It seems that throughout her work Diallo has reproduced an image of the family that is a reflection of her own or that represents her ideal. The girl is allowed to make certain basic choices herself and is given the freedom and incentive to develop her talents and pursue her own happiness.

Position of Women

Although Diallo puts special emphasis on the role of the family, she primarily focuses on the situation of women through her protagonists. Bruner considers *De Tilène au Plateau* important because of its portrayal of the female condition: "Diallo's autobiography is interesting in what she reveals, consciously and unconsciously, about Senegalese women today" (339). Roger Dorsinville comments that for the first time in African literature we find the story of a girl who imposes her own choices on her family (148). It has already been seen how the character and personality of Diallo's protagonists contribute to their success. They are all highly motivated, self-reliant, and individualistic. Diallo also reveals her feminist intent in the aspects of their lives that she chooses to underline. Thus education is an important central theme and an area in which all the main characters play an innovative role. The first girl allowed by her grandfather to go to school, Safi is a brilliant pupil, continuing to high school where there are very few girls. Her interest wanes, however, as she becomes preoccupied with the failing health of both her father and grandmother. Uncertain about a career, Safi finally takes the first available competitive examination, the one for midwives. Her vocation soon develops, however, and she graduates first in her class. Thiane's situation is different because the only formal schooling in traditional life was the teaching of the Coran. Yet, like Safi, Thiane is an exceptional student. At the age of ten she becomes the youngest person ever in her village to recite the whole Coran by heart. Fary's achievements are also related to the skills of traditional life. She looks after the sheep, a responsibility normally allotted to boys, and becomes the first girl to accompany the flock annually offered to the prince. Although she cannot prove herself in a school situation, Fary is constantly shown to be more perceptive and judicious than her peers. In *Awa La Petite Marchande* Diallo stresses the importance of formal education in modern Senegal. Awa calls school the last hope of the poor (49), and her parents do everything to encourage her studies. Yet before school she goes to the beach for the division of the fish catch, contrasting her life with that of most of her classmates, fresh from their beds. All of the poor girls in the class work hard and all are highly successful. Awa is unhappy to leave and eager to resume school when she goes to France. She continues on her return to Senegal and her future seems bright. Diallo thus presents us with four protagonists with exceptional intellectual gifts. An unequivocal advocate of education for girls, she shows them to be not merely the intellectual equals of boys but even their superiors.

Another central theme illuminating Diallo's desire for specific changes in the female condition is the relationship between the sexes and the question of freedom in marriage. In Wolof society, unlike many other African communities, girls are expected to remain virgins before marriage and a close watch is kept on their contact with boys. Traditionally marriage is an arrangement between two families rather than two individuals. From an early age Safi is taught to beware of boys. Her grandmother tells her that even their smell could make her pregnant, and she examines Safi's washing every month between puberty and marriage. Yet Safi sees her boyfriend regularly despite her father's opposition. Everyone except him considers them engaged, but Safi, her heart almost broken, terminates the relationship when she realizes his faults. This crisis is presented as the moment of transition from childhood to adulthood. Later she falls in love with someone else, having forgotten that she had meanwhile become engaged to another man away in France. Determined to marry the man of her final choice, she eventually succeeds. Yet it is significant that her future husband comes from a suitable family. She marries with a dowry but, to the horror of her aunts, without the customary watch and sewing machine. Nevertheless, Safi is given an extraordinary amount of freedom with regard to marriage. Most unusually, she chooses a husband for herself not once but three times.

Thiane is not prepared to accept the decision of others about her marital future either, and her parents are tolerant enough to allow her this liberty. Because of her great beauty Thiane's fame spreads beyond the boundaries of Cayor, but she refuses all her suitors. It is said that another girl would have been forced by her father to marry (58). Finally Thiane falls in love and her engagement is about to be celebrated when Cayor is invaded. In this way Thiane, like Safi, selects her own husband. Yet, although surprising in a traditional context, once again her fiancé is a suitable partner in terms of his family and religious background.

Fary too displays a remarkable lack of submissiveness in her relationships with men. When she visits the court as a shepherd girl, the prince sends her off alone to await his pleasure, but she rejoins her father and they return home without further incident. Fary is the first girl to reject the ruler's advances. She is in love with a handsome young man in the village, but chooses the prince for the altruistic reasons already mentioned. Her family does not force her into the marriage. The decision is entirely her own.

In *Awa la petite marchande,* the question of Awa's associations with the opposite sex does not arise because she is so young. The reader has no knowledge of her father's ideas on a suitable husband, but he is ill at ease with the emancipation of Awa's life in France. Nevertheless, one assumes that Diallo would again favor free choice for Awa. In her other works she shows that women should be at liberty to marry whom they wish and that normally love should be the deciding factor.

Although the situation of the protagonists is fortunate, the same cannot always be said of the other female characters. *De Tilène au Plateau* is full of women in minor roles. Apart from Mame, treated in detail, there are Safi's aunts, her sisters, her friends, and her women teachers. The reader learns very little about the lives of these women, except for Safi's cousin, Ami, whose courtship and marriage are the only other ones mentioned in the book. Ami's husband wins her hand because he is more generous with his prospective family-in-law than the other suitors. Security is put before love and Ami sees her marriage as an escape from a boring and sometimes oppressive life. The difference in freedom between Safi and Ami is presented as a matter of fact, without much commentary. At ease with the status quo, Diallo is certainly no militant feminist in her autobiography. She declines to question some social practices often considered detrimental to women, such as polygamy. Presented as the norm in her family, at least for the older generation, polygamy is never depicted as a source of conflict.

Le Fort maudit presents a different point of view. In this novel polygamy is problematic. It does not work. Despite the efforts of Thiane's father, Ibra, to establish harmony, his polygamous family is torn apart by rivalry, jealousy and the lack of intimacy between Ibra and his secondary wives. He is forced to repudiate his third wife when he discovers her repeated infidelity. One episode in the description of traditional life is particularly illuminating with regard to the theme of polygamy. Ibra, as the *kangam* or representative of the king, is called upon to sit in public judgement over a family dispute between the two wives of an old man. The younger wife, Farma, after swearing on the Coran, proceeds to talk arrogantly and contemptuously about what she would do to her older co-wife if she got the chance (40). The assembly is horrified at this never-before-seen act of defiance in front of the *kangam*. When Ibra talks of punishment, she slaps his face. Diallo may wish to show that the stereotype of the submissive woman in traditional life does not take into account the variety of attitudes and temperaments existing in every society and age. Nevertheless, this behavior seems highly improbable. Yet the incident, like the description of Ibra's family life, reveals the potentially destructive effects of polygamy on women. In the different situation of the fort, Farma becomes compassionate and self-sacrificing.

Le Fort maudit illustrates the dissensions within a polygamous family, but polygamy does not destroy Thiane's or her mother's happiness because they are the favorites. The first part of *La Princesse de Tiali*, however, presents a profoundly unhappy household. Polygamy greatly increases the hardships of village life and repudiation is the automatic reaction to revolt. At court, the prince's four wives devote most of their time and energy to protecting or advancing their own position in relation to that of their co-wives. A new dimension is added with the machinations of the queen-mother. Before Fary's arrival, she is the most influential woman in Tiali. Fary enjoys an unassailable position as favorite princess, but it is only maintained by combining persuasion with apparent submission. Only one woman in the novel stands out as a symbol of open female emancipation. Sokhna is divorced and of uncertain reputation, but she is powerful and wealthy because she can predict the future with her cowry shells. Strikingly beautiful, she has many suitors and eventually marries the one of her choice. Yet it is doubtful whether Sokhna could please herself if her special gifts did not make her largely invulnerable.

In *Awa la petite marchande*, polygamy is common within the clan and is indirectly condemned. So is the marriage of girls to older men, the case of Awa's friend, Yaba, being presented with regret. Although Awa's family is monogamous, the rise in their standard of living casts a shadow over the future happiness of Yacine at the end of the novel: "Allait-elle connaître la vie infernale de la polygamie?" (125). [Was she going to know the hell of polygamy?] In general, however, women are subject to the same social pressures as men and, like them, are presented as both victims and victimizers. More importantly than gender, social status confers or denies power.

Portrayal of Society

The portrayal of society is central to Diallo's work. Although Safi is not quite the ordinary Senegalese Diallo claims to be in her preface, certain aspects of her life are typical. She grows up in a devout polygamous extended family and religious belief is of primary importance in her life. She is also at pains to provide cultural information relevant to the lives of all Senegalese. This endeavor is evident in the descriptions of practices relating to circumcision and marriage, as well as the account of the exorcism ceremony. Her attitude is not always positive. She condemns the parasitism and greed associated with funerals, the vituperation of the old ladies against unmarried mothers, and the role money plays in the choice of a husband. Nevertheless, in the book as a whole there is a minimum of social criticism.

There is also no evidence of cultural conflict, although most of *De Tilène au Plateau* describes life before Independence. Not only is colonialism never condemned. It is never mentioned as such. European influences on young people are described honestly and without guilt. All the latest dances from Europe are the rage, as are the students home from France. Safi admires western dress and at one point is in despair because she has only African clothes. Safi's first European primary teacher is presented positively and even Safi's school prize, a doll with blond curls, is not interpreted as a negative symbol. When she leaves for France with her husband, no comment is made from the point of view of the clash of cultures. It seems that for Diallo this conflict did not exist.

Surprisingly, although one of Diallo's major aims as stated in her preface is the portrayal of a disappearing world, the friction between traditions and modernity is not a major theme. It is represented mainly through the generation conflict between Safi and her father over her first boyfriend. Yet at the beginning of the book Diallo mentions her nostalgia for the honesty, mutual respect, and piety she claims were more common during her childhood. She also places particular emphasis on a disappearing sense of honor, which, she stresses, was not an imported virtue but an age-old ideal communicated over the centuries through stories and legends. This remark seems to be directed both to Senegalese readers and to any Westerners who might be tempted to think that virtue was brought by the colonizing power. In general, however, there is little harking back to better times, except when Diallo talks of her dead father and grandmother. Nor are the moral overtones always there, for sometimes she simply states that a custom has changed.

As has been mentioned, the positive depiction of traditional society is without doubt one of the main aims of Diallo in *Le Fort maudit*. Sahel relates the work to the constant search for identity in African literature, calling the novel the spiritual biography of a tree looking for its roots (64). The annual market is described in detail, as well as the way in which Thiane and her mother prepare themselves for this important outing. So too are all the activities at the *damel*'s court. Another prominent episode is the public ceremony where Ibra's niece has her lips tattooed before her marriage. These sequences are presumably included to make the re-creation of traditional existence both more realistic and more interesting and to show that life before the arrival of the Europeans was not restricted to grinding millet and working the fields.

Although Islam plays a primary role in the work, the attitude to religion is ambivalent at the end. With his dying breath Ibra tells his daughter to keep her faith in God, whatever happens (93). Yet Thiane loses her religious faith and, despite the prayers and sacrifices, Islamic Cayor is defeated by pagan Baol. Thiane's vengeance and death are not placed in a religious context, despite the use of the word "martyre" in the prologue. Her role as a tragic heroine is flawed because it is linked more closely to her personal hate than to the cause of her people and religion.

Unlike *Le Fort maudit*, *La Princesse de Tiali* attacks some aspects of traditional life surviving into modern times, while at the same time it destroys the romantic idea of village life. It is the Wolof caste system, however, that is the main object of Diallo's criticism. Fary's village was established by *griots*, a low caste, but she refuses a classification that takes away her full dignity as a human being. Her marriage to the prince, normally considered an impossible union, is the first stage in Fary's fight for the rehabilitation of her people. Because of her intervention the prince gives *griots* full participatory rights in the assembly and in the cabinet. The work ends with Fary's vow to continue working for her people.

This novel also appears to condemn the power of the *marabouts* (holy men) through the role of Serigne Tierno, instrumental in persuading the queen-mother to accept her son's marriage to Fary. His cupidity is boundless and his success has nothing to do with supernatural powers but rather with his intelligent use of the information he receives from the different participants in the drama. Yet the importance of Islam is never questioned. Fary's first significant act after her marriage is to convert the prince. Another major episode in the novel is the struggle of the villagers to obtain permission to bury their dead the Islamic way. When it is finally obtained, Fary's mother can die in peace.

The degrading and sometimes ruinous distribution of gifts at ceremonies is highlighted in Diallo's description of the baptism of Fary's first son. Although money did not exist, the exchange of goods is shown to be a hypocritical attempt to humiliate the other side of the family, rather than a genuine show of generosity.

Awa la petite marchande is also highly critical of Senegalese society, but the modern setting makes the criticism more direct. The main division is between rich and poor and once again there is a dichotomy in that the rich are bad and the poor are good. Awa and her family are shown to be honest and virtuous. Their more affluent enemies are petty, malicious, and sometimes corrupt. By creating a poor heroine, Diallo reveals all the injustices suffered by the underprivileged. Awa's parents are even victimized by their own relatives, particularly by Aunt Sala, the first wife of the head of the extended family. At school there are the same divisions, although there is greater solidarity among the poor. Physical attributes represent moral superiority or inferiority. The rich girls are all fat and ugly. During the gymnastics class "ces grosses filles suffoquaient à perdre haleine, tombaient, s'écrasaient sur le sol comme des fruits mûrs" (52). [these fat girls almost suffocated from lack of breath, fell, and squashed themselves on the floor like ripe fruit.] Awa and her friends sit on the right, the position for the best pupils. Her rich cousin, Rama, and company sit on the left with the worst pupils. One day, however, Rama moves to the middle, the classroom has new equipment and the teacher is wearing new clothes. Rama tells her friends that she brings the teacher an envelope from her father every day (46). In this society, money is the key to success. One of the most important episodes in the book describes the religious song festival, an excuse for the rich to exhibit their wealth and a reason for the poor to attempt to imitate them. Although Diallo is critical of the hypocrisy sometimes associated with religion, she never casts doubt on the validity of true religious belief. Diallo has Awa affirm her faith on the boat to France, where the beauty of the sunset reminds her of her own insignificance and of the omnipotence of God (98).

Contrary to the accepted idea about the solidarity of the African extended family, *Awa la petite marchande* shows it to be dominated by selfishness and lack of compassion. Salif's illness reveals the spitefulness and indifference of Awa's aunts and uncles. Yet Diallo is anxious to show the importance of friendship. The neighbor, Mame Sira, and her nephew, Kader, are devoted to Awa's family. Mame Sira is a wise and pious grandmother-figure, a Malian despised as a foreigner in Senegal. She in turn considers the Senegalese too proud and obsessed with shame. Kader is an important public servant with a degree from France. Ironically, he seems to be a "toubab noir" ("Black European"). Yet he is the one who helps Awa's family in their time of crisis.

Diallo does not link the cruelty and egoism she depicts to the influence of European individualism. If *Awa la petite marchande* is related to the historical *La Princesse de Tiali*, where the villagers are petty, selfish, and totally unworthy of Fary's sacrifices, it is evident that in Diallo's opinion Senegalese society always had these flaws. It is not possible to tie the largely negative view of society to a conflict between tradition and modernity. Diallo's positive description of life in France infers that she is in favor of progress. The metamorphosis within Salif and also in Yacine indicates that an escape from poverty is the necessary precondition for contentment. Grinding poverty takes away the potential for personal development. Diallo's didactic intent is clear. She shows through the reversal of fortunes in the family that virtue and hard work are rewarded, while ill-doing is punished.

All Diallo's writing reflects her dual interest in the female condition and in social norms, but her point of view is not always the same. In *De Tilène au Plateau* the feminist intent is either unconscious or discreet. Safi would appear to be a role model and a representative of her culture, but the situation of women in general is not treated directly. Ironically, Safi's progress mirrors the social transition away from a way of life Diallo is anxious to record. In the following three novels there is a conscious feminism apparent in the choice of a protagonist embodying specific virtues to be admired and perhaps imitated. In the case of Thiane, her characterization is an integral part of the evocation of the cultural richness and moral rectitude of pre-colonial Islamic Africa. Fary is equally heroic but in *La Princesse de Tiali* a contrast is created between the virtues of the protagonist and the insufficiencies of her society. Although Thiane and Fary are apparently fictitious, readers could take them to be historical figures, thereby strengthening their influence as role models. In *Awa la petite marchande*, the feminist intent in the choice of a young girl as heroine is placed in the context of general social problems overshadowing the individual destiny of the protagonist. Diallo seems to have a triple purpose in writing this book. First, she is presenting Awa as a model for other children, particularly girls, to show that hard work at home and at school and devotion to the family bring their reward. Related to this is her desire to arouse sympathy and understanding for poverty and to advocate education as a means of escape. (Although it is hard to see how Salif and Awa could have succeeded without going to France, one hesitates to interpret the book as a recommendation that those who have problems in Senegal should follow their example.) Finally, Diallo uses the story as a vehicle for criticism of a society where corruption, selfishness, and snobbery are the ruling forces, even within the extended family.

Diallo's heroines correspond closely to what Beatrice Stegeman calls "the new woman" in African literature. Each has the energy and determination to reach her goals and, except for Fary, believes in the ideals of life, liberty, and personal happiness. Each uses her reason and assumes a responsibility for her future that Stegeman says is absent from the lives of traditional African women. Diallo, however, claims through the characters of Thiane and Fary that in reality this is not a "new woman" but a type who has always existed, even if out of the ordinary. She apparently counters the claim that western feminism has improved the situation of African women and asserts her independence from western feminist trends.

The autobiographical element remains strong throughout Diallo's writing. Her heroines are in part projections of herself, if we take Safi as a reference, in the same way that the immediate family relationships in the later works reflect Diallo's closeness to her father and grandmother. Although Diallo came from a relatively privileged family, she is aware that the situation of most Senegalese women is different. In her last two works, much more critical of social limitations on both men and women than her autobiography, she reveals her desire for change. She is anxious, however, that improved educational opportunities and increased freedom of choice should not destroy the power of religion and the importance of the family.

III

Mariama Bâ

In 1979 Mariama Bâ published *Une Si Longue Lettre*. It caused such a stir that one can only assume it represented the revelation about Black African women that the world had been waiting for. Blair calls it "the first truly feminist African novel" (139) and Guyonneau says in the introduction to her bibliography, "The success of Mariama Bâ's novel . . . has heralded, it seems, a new era for African women writers" (453). In 1980 it received the first Noma award for the best overseas novel in French because, according to the chairperson of the selection panel, Eldred Jones, it "offers a testimony of the female condition in Africa while at the same time giving that testimony true imaginative depth" (Harrell-Bond 2). Aminata Maïga Ka, a writer herself and a friend and compatriot of Bâ's, also emphasizes her role as a torchbearer for women (134). Thus, unlike Nafissatou Diallo, Bâ was immediately perceived as a feminist writer, and this facet of her work has attracted universal attention. Her second novel, *Un Chant écarlate*, published a few months after her death in 1981, is not so openly feminist. It appears to be a deliberate attempt to present a multiplicity of viewpoints, both male and female, and therefore a more general social view.

Bâ outlined her views on the role of African writers in a published article entitled "La Fonction politique des littératures africaines écrites." They should awaken the conscience of the reader and serve as a guide, while avoiding the production of social or political tracts. A work of art must be a harmonious blending of commitment and artistic values. At the end of the article Bâ refers specifically to women and gives her explanation, presented in chapter 1, for the hesitancy of all women, and African women in particular, about publishing. She claims that women who protest are despised and marginalized in all cultures, making them afraid of expressing themselves in print. Yet, she concludes passionately, it is the duty of African women not just to write, but to use writing as an arm to destroy the age-old oppression of their sex: "Les chants nostalgiques dédiés à la mère africaine confondue dans les angoisses d'homme à la Mère Afrique ne nous suffisent plus" (7). [Nostalgic songs dedicated to the African mother mixed up with male anguish about Mother Africa are no longer enough for us.] She does not forget the problem of literacy and the controversy over the use of European languages. She writes in French because it is the only written language she knows, and, although she introduces very little Wolof into her text, she recognizes the need for the promotion of writing in African languages so that literature can reach a wider public.

In the light of Mariama Bâ's stated feminist aims, the basic question to ask about her writing is how those aims are reflected in the form and content of her two novels.

Feminism, Form and Content

Une Si Longue Lettre is a first-person account of the trials and tribulations of Ramatoulaye, a middle-aged, middle-class Senegalese woman. It begins in a sense where Nafissatou Diallo's *De Tilène au Plateau* ends, with the higher education of the two main characters and their marriage, highlighting the different emphases in the two works. Whereas Diallo is anxious to recreate the Dakar of her childhood and to show us the forces shaping her early life, Bâ is more interested in the relationships between men and women and the problems a mature woman faces in present-day Senegal.

Although it is called a letter, it is not an epistolary novel in the strict or traditional sense, defined by Ruth Perry in the following way:

Epistolary fiction always works according to a formula: two or more people, separated by an obstruction . . . are forced to maintain their relationship through letters. This genre . . . runs on the tension of one or both of these separate characters trying to surmount the obstacles between them in order to be finally united (93).

This is not true of *Une Si Longue Lettre*. It begins: "Aïssatou, J'ai reçu ton mot" [Dear Aïssatou, I have received your letter[8]] but the narrator does not send what she is writing. There are no letters as such and Aïssatou is actually a silent interlocutor. Later in the novel, the narrator mentions receiving another letter from her, but this letter does not affect the development of the narrative except perhaps to encourage the narrator. As is now recognized by most critics, the book is more like a personal diary addressed ostensibly to a life-long friend, a diary, covering both past and present, but primarily written while the narrator is going through the four months and ten day mourning period decreed by Islam. It opens with the news of the death of the narrator's husband, Modou, and his funeral. This introduction is followed by a long flashback covering more than one third of the book (24–83), beginning when the narrator is training to be a teacher and continuing to her marriage and its eventual failure. The last section returns to the present, that is, to the events in Ramatoulaye's life at the end of her official mourning period. The writing of the diary can be considered a form of therapy similar to that described in Miriam Warner-Vieyra's *Juletane* (1982), also set partly in Senegal. In this novel a woman believed to be mentally unbalanced tries to come to terms with her situation and relieve her solitude by writing everything down. The narrator in *Une Si Longue Lettre* also has to face her solitude in the sequestration following her husband's death and to resolve her state of psychological and emotional confusion. In this sense, Bâ's novel does have much in common with the epistolary novel as analyzed by Perry: "What the characters enact in their seclusion is at the core of the epistolary novel: a self-conscious and self-perpetuating process of emotional self-examination which gathers momentum and ultimately becomes more important than communicating

with anyone outside the room in which one sits alone writing letters"
(117). Although Ramatoulaye often addresses Aïssatou directly, her
thoughts sometimes seem more directed to herself. She says she chooses
her friend because they grew up together and Aïssatou has shared many
of the experiences described or has suffered the same ordeals. One of the
underlying assertions of the book is that friendship is stronger than
romantic love. Aïssatou functions as a double to Ramatoulaye and is
often described by critics as her alter ego. This interpretation strengthens
the idea of *Une Si Longue Lettre* as a meditation directed at the person
closest to her. When it recounts the past, the narrative is like a protracted
conversation between two people where one of the speakers needs to
talk, and the other person is prepared to listen, even though she has
heard it all before. Ramatoulaye makes this point in chapter 4 when she
implicitly apologizes for boring her friend with what she already knows.
Yet she also informs Aïssatou about what is happening around her in the
immediate present, as Aïssatou lives and works abroad. Ramatoulaye
often imagines her friend's response to what she is writing: "tu me
diras" [you may tell me] or "tu me répondras" [you may reply]. By
writing to someone, the narrator finds it easier to express her inner
conflicts and sufferings, for although this is not a genuine letter, she
intends to show it to Aïssatou when she arrives on a visit the day after
the "diary" ends. Thus, F. I. Case's assertion that the "neutralization of
the named addressee, Aïssatou, nullifies the letter and its purpose and
makes nonsense of the work" (539) is not valid.

Nor is Aïssatou the only addressee. Chapter six (a little over two
pages) is largely written to Modou, revealing that Ramatoulaye's "diary"
is a reliving of the past so that she can come to terms with it, rather than
a series of letters to which she expects constructive answers. In chapter
17, at the end of the flashback, the narrator summarizes her attempts to
create a happy marriage and a happy home, concluding: "Et je
m'interroge. Et je m'interroge. Pourquoi? Pourquoi Modou s'est-il
détaché? Pourquoi a-t-il introduit Binetou entre nous?" (83) [And I ask
myself. I ask myself? Why did Modou detach himself? Why did he put

Binetou between us? (56)]. By mentally reliving her life with her husband, Ramatoulaye hopes to arrive at an understanding of his betrayal. It is a painful process. Past happiness serves to underline her recent suffering and present loss. She does, however, remember the joys of her early relationship with Modou with tenderness and nostalgia, resulting in some of the most lyrical passages of the novel.

There is often a dramatic tension between what is happening inside and outside Ramatoulaye. This contrast serves to illuminate the position of women in her society in that her thoughts and emotions conflict with the role she is forced to play because of social conventions. Reading her account is like entering a secret world hidden from those around her. The disparity between external appearances and inner reality is particularly striking in two episodes. The first is at Modou's funeral, where, although she is full of resentment both towards her dead husband and her rapacious family-in-law, Ramatoulaye is forced to play the role of the meek and devoted widow and sister-in-law. She is obliged to comply with the duties and impositions associated with funerals, while abhorring the exhibitionism and lack of piety around her. If she did reveal her inner revolt, it would probably be misconstrued as a revolt against religion. In addition, she is too confused and exhausted to react other than in writing.

The second episode in which she hides her true feelings is in her account of the past and is particularly revealing of the behavior and attitude of women towards men. In chapter 13 she describes the visit of the all-male delegation sent by Modou to inform her that he has taken a second wife. Suffering from shock at the totally unexpected news, but determined not to give these men the satisfaction of seeing her distress, Ramatoulaye makes a superhuman effort to reveal nothing of her inner reactions. She smiles and thanks them. She smiles and serves te nauseated by the smell of the wedding incense still clinging to visitors. As the narrator says, her reaction is partly dictated by pride African rules of hospitality as well as a belief in the privacy of s emotions also influence her behavior.

As the novel progresses, it becomes clear that the therapy is taking effect. Ramatoulaye slowly begins to deal with Modou's betrayal and abandonment. At first, as she attempts to carry out the process of inner purification dictated by religion, she admits that her memories have a bitter taste. After the fortieth day of mourning she claims that she has forgiven her husband (chapter 18.) At the opening of the diary Ramatoulaye refers to the Islamic practice of *Mirasse* dictated by the Coran. This requirement entails listing the possessions of the deceased in order to divide the inheritance. By its very nature, the process involves the revelation of the most intimate details of the person's life. This concept of *Mirasse* can be extended to the whole novel and applied to Ramatoulaye's quest for order, perspective, and inner peace. In the last words of the novel, Ramatoulaye shows that she has laid the ghost of her past and can look forward to her future with hope. She is determined to be happy: "C'est de l'humus sale et nauséabond que jaillit la plante verte et je sens pointer en moi des bourgeons neufs" (131). [It is from the dirty and nauseating humus that the green plant sprouts into life, and I can feel new buds springing up in me (89)]. The process of purgation and renewal is complete. The diary has fulfilled its purpose d is brought to an end with the narrator's signature. The diary form of novel is fundamental to Bâ's feminist intent. Feminism is presented natter of consciousness. It is an inward process occurring through ights and feelings of the individual woman. The diary form is ay of exteriorizing that inwardness without losing any of its d a means of creating a strong emotional bond between and the reader.

he first-person narrative and the confidential tone of *Une* it is often referred to as an autobiographical novel. Aminata Maïga Ka, feels there was a strong uence. She relates in her article on this novel how laye to the author at a public talk in Senegal at present. Bâ avoided the issue by retorting that ness nor greatness of spirit of Ramatoulaye

(134). She denied in an interview (Bruner 1983) that either of the main characters was a self-portrait, for although she was divorced, she had had a monogamous marriage. She claimed that her characters were composites of contemporary educated Senegalese women (32). Despite these denials, there are a number of clear links between Bâ and her narrator. They are both fifty in 1979 when the novel was published. Like Bâ, Ramatoulaye was an elementary school teacher and studied at the teachers' college in Rufisque, near Dakar. Bâ came first in French West Africa in the competitive examination for entry to that institution and points out that she was the first in her family to "do things differently" (Harrell-Bond 3). In chapter 6 Ramatoulaye reminds Aïssatou that they were among the first few pioneers of the promotion of African women. Bâ belonged to an important family, her father being the first Minister of Health after the decentralization bill of 1956 (Loi cadre). Ramatoulaye mentions that she comes from one of the most important families in Dakar. She has twelve children, whereas Bâ had only nine, but both families are very large. Like Ramatoulaye, Bâ still believed in marriage as a viable and fundamental social institution, even after her divorce (Harrell-Bond). Bâ's mother died, however, when she was very young, which is not the case with Ramatoulaye, whose mother was still alive at the time of her marriage. Furthermore, there is a device within the novel itself that makes it appear to be autobiography. The narrator's name is not revealed to be different from that of the author until two-thirds through the book. As Philippe Lejeune points out in his *Le Pacte autobiographique*, that pact is largely based on the author and the narrator of a work using the same name. Until the two are separated in *Une Si Longue Lettre,* the reader assumes them to be one and the same.

Paradoxically, this anonymity also means that the narrator becomes *the* Senegalese woman abandoned for another woman after many years of marriage. She becomes representative of the many women who have suffered the same fate. When Ramatoulaye is trying to decide how to react to Modou's second marriage, she begins to count all the women she knows who have been abandoned or divorced. That Bâ's countrywomen took her narrator to be representative is clear from the declaration of another Senegalese woman writer, Mame Seck Mbacke, when she was interviewed for French radio. She says that every Senegalese woman sees herself in Bâ's novel. She tells how many women went to see Bâ after publication and told the author that they were astonished to discover that her book was a faithful recreation of their own experiences. It is a major achievement of this novel that it succeeds in appearing to be both a personal autobiography and a general account of the feminine condition in Senegal. This dual accomplishment may be responsible for its enormous impact.

Whether one calls *Une Si Longue Lettre* an autobiographical novel or a pseudo-autobiography, Bâ gives herself more freedom by creating a separate narrator. There is a parallel here with Cheik Hamidou Kane's use in *Une Aventure ambiguë* of his own Peulh name (Samba) for his narrator. The uninformed reader does not recognize the connection, and, as Bernadette Cailler points out, the author has complete freedom of expression within the novel form (747). Nevertheless, she concludes that Kane's work is primarily autobiography. Serge Doubrovsky makes the same point in an article on his own "autofiction," *Fils*, where he is both author and narrator. By calling his work a novel, he is released from any attempt to present the whole "truth," an impossible task anyway, as an autobiography can only present one of a number of possible "truths." Bâ too is able to use all the devices available to the creative writer, while seeming to draw primarily on her own life. She is not restricted to factual accuracy, nor can be accused of fabrication, yet the reader feels that *Une Si Longue Lettre* is a true story and therefore finds it more inspiring.

While primarily using a (pseudo)autobiographical approach or first-person narrative, Bâ at the same time introduces techniques normally associated with freer forms of fiction. First, the narrator sometimes appears to be replaced by an omniscient author. Ramatoulaye presents Tante Nabou's desire for revenge against her daughter-in-law, Aïssatou, as though she knew about it at the time, an impossibility because of the nature of her relationship with the older woman. Another example of this change of roles is in the account of Tante Nabou's journey back to the village. In that episode, the reader witnesses both the thoughts and even the words of the old lady: "'Pour se convaincre de la survie des traditions, il faut sortir de Dakar', murmurait Tante Nabou" (44). ['You have to come away from Dakar to be convinced of the survival of traditions,' murmured Aunty Nabou (27)]. The same device is used with Binetou, Modou's second wife: the narrator comments that the image of her destroyed life was breaking Binetou's heart (ch. 15). In this case the narrator says that her daughter, Daba, went to the same places, but Daba did not speak to Binetou and had no way of knowing her thoughts. When Aïssatou chooses divorce rather than a polygamous marriage and tells her husband in a letter, Ramatoulaye says she remembers the exact contents and reproduces it in full. This could be considered too blatant a move from narrator to omniscient author. For Christopher Miller, however, these deviations from European literary norms are at the heart of the novel. He considers that Bâ asserts her freedom as an African woman writer to both borrow and reject, resulting in what Miller calls "an original act of literary creativity, a brilliant departure" (283). Nevertheless, the reader may feel that these occasional changes in point of view break the continuity of the narrative.

The second technique normally related to fiction rather than autobiography is the way in which Bâ uses the first person narrative to represent different perspectives. Elizabeth Mudimbe-Boyi says that the author pretends to echo multiple voices but that there is actually only one authoritative voice, that of the narrator. Yet the point of view in the novel can be interpreted conversely as one voice in reality representing many. Thus, for different reasons, I agree with Mudimbe-Boyi's formula of one character with multiple voices and with her categorization of these multiple voices as follows: the letter's writer, Senegalese women, African women, all women, the spouse, the mother and, lastly, men who support women's emancipation. Despite the very personal tones of the novel and the clear autobiographical references, the characters are clearly types, as Bâ herself claims. In the Harrell-Bond interview, she said *Une Si Longue Lettre* was a cry from the heart of all women, although first and foremost from that of Islamic Senegalese women. This combination of the personal and the general is basic to the novel's feminist approach.

The apparent identification with one point of view is rejected in Bâ's second novel, *Un Chant écarlate*. It presents an omniscient author who reveals the hearts and minds of all the characters, although primarily those of the protagonists, the Frenchwoman, Mireille, and the Senegalese man, Ousmane. Superficially, Mireille's function is merely that of catalyst to Ousmane's identity crisis as an African who has betrayed his origins by marrying a white woman. The story is fundamentally the same as in *Une Si Longue Lettre*: a couple marry for love but later the man turns to another woman and takes her as his second wife. The first wife is then forced to choose her reaction. The problems are compounded by a racially mixed marriage. In the Harrell-Bond interview Bâ explains that she chose a marriage between an African man and a European wife because a white daughter-in-law is problematic in the Senegalese context where she is traditionally absorbed into the husband's family.

One is not immediately aware of the similarities between Bâ's two novels because of the multiplicity of viewpoints and the resulting complexity of the narrative, making *Un Chant écarlate* an apparently richer work. Yet the reader is not allowed to identify closely with any character. Almost all are presented more negatively than positively as the novel progresses, so that the reader remains emotionally detached. This second novel is therefore not as powerful or absorbing as Bâ's first. Blair (1984) calls it a "roman à thèse" and says that "the author has contrived a situation to accommodate her thesis and then created characters to act out the morality to its melodramatic dénouement" (139). She thinks that the subject of mixed marriages is a trap for the writer because of the temptation to fall into stereotypes.

Bâ originally thought of calling the novel "Le tertre abandonné" in reference to a Wolof proverb: "When one abandons one's own hillock, any hillock one climbs will crumble" (information given by Blair among others). Two references are made to this proverb in the text itself: when Ousmane's mother, Yaye Khady, talks of Mireille as the white woman who came down from her own hill to intrude into the world of black people (II,2) and on the last page where Ousmane's father quotes the proverb in Wolof followed by the French translation. Perhaps Bâ thought her original title too obvious and for that reason changed it to the more intriguing *Un Chant écarlate*. The title appears in the text at the end when a scarlet song of lost hopes is said to rise out of Ousmane's wounds.

This novel is not only about one's roots and a love affair that turns to tragedy. It is also about growing up in a poor area of Dakar. The urban environment is more important here than in *Une Si Longue Lettre*, where the action really takes place inside the narrator's mind. The text is explicitly divided into three parts. The opening three chapters constitute a flashback describing Ousmane's childhood and youth in the form of his thoughts as he walks for the first time to the university. The rest of the first part deals with the relationship between Mireille and Ousmane, both in Senegal and later as they write to each other between Senegal and France. The second part describes the return to Africa of the young couple after their wedding in Paris and the steady deterioration of their marriage. Part three narrates Ousmane's retreat to his origins, to his old neighborhood and to his childhood sweetheart, Ouleymatou, whom he eventually marries without telling Mireille. Her discovery of this second marriage and her inability to cope with the transfer of Ousmane's love leads to insanity. She kills their baby and attempts to kill her husband. The novel closes on this note of despair.

Once again a woman is badly treated by her husband. He turns away from their marriage and looks for solutions to his life in his relationship with a second wife. This time, however, the woman does not come out of the ordeal strengthened as an individual, able to assume responsibility for her own existence. Mireille can see no remedy. Returning to France seems impossible because of her parents' rejection and the racism her son would encounter, so the situation destroys her. In this novel the perspective is no longer exclusively female. Ousmane's viewpoint is primordial, and even if he finally loses the reader's sympathy, we are able to understand his thoughts and feelings in a way impossible with Modou or Mawdo in *Une Si Longue Lettre*. The difference in form appears to represent an attempt by Bâ to avoid two of the basic elements of her first novel: ostensible autobiographical content and what could be considered a one-sided militant feminism that fails to recognize the pressures on all Africans, both men and women, in a rapidly changing world.

Victims and Victimizers

The central theme of both Bâ's novels is the search for happiness within the couple relationship as expressed in a monogamous marriage. That this search generally results in failure is due principally to male polygamous instincts, but the influence of the family and cultural conflict are important contributory causes in the case of Mireille and Ousmane. Despite Ojo-Ade's criticism of what he calls the extreme and distorted feminism in *Une Si Longue Lettre* based on a totally negative view of men and the opposite of women, Bâ distinctly shows that she is not positing a simple equivalence of man as victimizer and woman as victim. Women are also victimizers of other women and partially responsible for their marital unhappiness. In the first novel, however, the two main characters, as well as a lesser, third character (Jacqueline) are presented as the victims of their husbands' lust and weakness. Aïssatou is the first to be faced with the problem of polygamy, brought about by the long-term machinations of her mother-in-law, but accepted without protest by her husband, Mawdo, who uses his mother as an excuse. Despite her husband's protestations of love, Aïssatou chooses divorce and makes a new life for herself overseas.

Ramatoulaye's twenty-five year old marriage to Modou was successful until he fell in love with Binetou, a friend of their daughter, Daba. Modou is a coward. Afraid to tell Ramatoulaye he has married again, he sends a delegation after the ceremony. The three men hypocritically use religion to justify the new union, conveniently referred to as the will of Allah, but when Ramatoulaye accepts polygamy, Modou abandons his first family, despite the Islamic decree that wives must be treated equally. The third example of a mistreated wife is that of Jacqueline. The six-page subplot is inserted into the long flashback, at the moment where Ramatoulaye is debating her reaction to the marriage with Binetou. The case of Jacqueline, a Protestant from the Ivory Coast, is particularly interesting to non-Africans. She is not accepted by the Senegalese and the narrator explicitly tells us (like Diallo through the character of the Malian, Mame Sire) that accepted ideas about the homogeneousness of Africa, often propagated by Africans themselves, are inaccurate. Her husband's open preference for Senegalese women and her general feeling of alienation lead to Jacqueline's illness, which she believes is purely physical. When a perceptive doctor explains the psychological cause, she acquires the strength to confront the situation positively, although the reader never learns the consequences. Bâ appears conscious that she could be accused of documentation with regard to the insertion about Jacqueline. Ramatoulaye asks herself why she is writing about her friend and concludes that it is a delaying tactic to avoid writing about her decision to accept polygamy.

The situation in *Un Chant écarlate* is more complex. Mireille is not presented as a victim in the same categorical way. First, Mireille shares the blame for the breakdown of her marriage. Second, the relationship is seen through the eyes of Ousmane too. In the first part of the book, he is presented positively as an exemplary son who puts his family first, even as a child. He is equally honorable in his relationship with Mireille, although the final decision to marry her is not made without a conflict within himself between his heart and his "society." Yet after the marriage he suddenly changes. In the rest of the novel he is negatively portrayed, despite explanations about his conduct that should make the reader sympathize with him. It is as though Bâ is doing her best to be fair to Ousmane, but cannot help revealing her own convictions about male sexual infidelity (Harrell-Bond interview.) Even his friend, Ali, who seems to represent Bâ's point of view, finds Ousmane's attitude towards Mireille uncompromising. When Ousmane begins a relationship with Ouleymatou unknown to his wife, Ali accuses him of sacrificing his honor and dignity, two qualities of major importance among traditional African virtues. Ousmane, like Modou, is revealed to be a coward. He decides to force Mireille to leave Senegal by making her life unbearable. To render his metamorphosis more believable to the reader, Bâ shows that Ousmane's friends are astonished by his behavior and consider the possibility of witchcraft. When Mireille goes mad, Ousmane suddenly understands what he has done and is overwhelmed with disgust. He has justified his conduct all along as a return to his true African self after being seduced by western values. Although the conflict is valid, in his case it seems more a tool of self-deception, used to disguise his sexual attraction to Ouleymatou and the death of his love for Mireille.

The final impression in the novel is that Mireille has been deeply wronged by Ousmane. She, like the three women in *Une Si Longue Lettre*, is the victim of her husband's selfishness and vanity. Or, to use Bâ's own words to Harrell-Bond, once again it is a case of a man indulging his polygamous instincts. It may be that Bâ began her novel with the idea of illustrating the Wolof proverb about leaving one's own hillock and finding no other refuge. She ended up communicating the same message as in her first novel. Or conversely, as Aminata Maïga Ka points out (134), her first novel also illustrates the proverb. In the three relationships described in *Une Si Longue Lettre*, the woman married outside her own group. Ramatoulaye married below her social class without the approval of her parents and without a dowry. Aïssatou married into a superior caste against the wishes of her mother-in-law. Jacqueline married a man from a different country and a different religion and broke with her family to do it. Ka argues that these women are all punished for defying tradition (134). Yet this interpretation does not seem to be the essential message of Bâ's novels. All four women are presented as victims of their male partners rather than of their own lack of judgment.

African men are not alone in their victimization of their wives. Madame de la Vallée, Mireille's mother, is the most oppressed female character in Bâ's novels. She has completely sacrificed her individuality to satisfy every whim of her autocratic husband, who also happens to be a hypocritical racist. When the news arrives that Mireille has married Ousmane, her immediate reaction is to forgive her daughter. Monsieur de la Vallée, however, is overcome by anger and calls his daughter a traitor and a slut. His wife then repeats his words, before she faints (II,3). If this imitative behavior was not so sad it would be funny. Mireille's mother is more in need of "liberation" than any of the African women Bâ portrays. Through this character the author shows that the problem of female self-determination is not confined to Africa.

In the Harrell-Bond interview Bâ rejects the claim that women in Africa have always been emancipated and asserts that their power has only been moral. She talks of a hidden mutual distrust between the sexes, claiming that Senegalese men like to choose their wife on the basis of the modern idea of romantic love, but then wish her to behave traditionally after marriage. Men are loath to abandon the privileges accorded to them in traditional society, particularly that of polygamy, opposed by Bâ on the grounds that it merely legalizes natural male infidelity. This theorizing links up with an interesting passage in *Un Chant écarlate* after Mireille's discovery of Ousmane's infidelity. It begins with the words: "A ses dépens, Mireille découvrait les fluctuations du désir chez l'homme" (237) [Mireille discovered to her cost the ebb and flow of man's desire (158)[9]]. What follows in the original French text (partly lost in the English translation) is a highly analytical passage on that theme, seeming to reflect Mireille's thoughts. Yet the tone and level of language are not those of Mireille so that it appears to be the voice of an outsider. This outsider is not, however, the omniscient author, who returns in the passage immediately following. As the language is that of an objective analyst, perhaps of a psychologist, the insertion may repeat what Mireille has read in her attempt to resolve her predicament. Even so, such an explanation would not explain the statement: "Rien de rationnel n'est

offert à mon investigation" (238). [My investigation has discovered no
rational explanation. My translation.] The words "mon investigation" do
not seem to belong to Mireille. The point of view in this passage remains
unclear, but it reveals once again both Bâ's fascination with male
infidelity and also her didactic intent. She presents marriage as an
institution that by its very nature demands more from the woman, who
must mold her life around that of the man, whether she has a career of
her own or not. In *Une Si Longue Lettre* Ramatoulaye writes: "Pour tout
dire, la réussite de chaque homme est assise sur un support féminin" (83)
[In a word, a man's success depends on feminine support (56)].

Nevertheless, men do not carry all the blame for failed marriages.
There is often a generation conflict within the family, normally
originating on the husband's side, as when a woman marries she enters
his family. Although Ramatoulaye's parents do not approve of her union
with Modou, they do not interfere. She is forced to go out of her way,
however, to placate Modou's female relatives. They do not try to wreck
the marriage, a good match for them, but they make onerous demands
on her time and purse. She avoids conflict by treating them like royalty,
especially her mother-in-law. Unfortunately for Aïssatou, her situation
is different because Mawdo belongs to the nobility and she is the
daughter of a goldsmith and therefore of an inferior caste. From the
beginning, her mother-in-law, Tante Nabou, sets out to destroy the
marriage with a long-term plan of vengeance. She invites her own niece
(of noble blood) to live with her and brings her up as the ideal traditional
wife. She then insists that Mawdo marry her. Tante Nabou is not
presented as an evil woman but as "cette mère rigide, pétrie de morale
ancienne, brûlée intérieurement par les féroces lois antiques" (48) [This
rigid mother molded by the old morality, burning with the fierce ardor
of antiquated laws (30)]. She is an anachronism in modern society, like
the caste system itself. The old woman's prejudices blind her to any
appreciation of Aïssatou virtues: "Une bijoutière, peut-elle avoir de la
dignité, de l'honneur?" (49). [Could a goldsmith's daughter have any
dignity, any honor? (31)]. For Tante Nabou the answer is clearly no, not

in comparison with a noblewoman. There are obvious similarities between her attitude to her daughter-in-law and that of Ousmane's mother, Yaye Khady, towards Mireille. Ousmane's father, although saddened by his son's marriage to a white woman, accepts it as the will of God. Yaye Khady, like Tante Nabou, sets out to change the situation. In her opinion a white woman can never be a proper daughter-in-law. There is some justification for her attitude, as traditionally Mireille would take over Yaye Khady's work. Yet she also refuses to accept Mireille as a full human being because she is white and makes no attempt to facilitate her integration into Senegalese society. She makes her life as difficult as possible and is largely supported in all she does by Ousmane, becoming an important contributory factor to the breakdown of the marriage. Despite the racial element in *Un Chant écarlate*, Bâ presents the problem of the mother-in-law as victimizer as a common phenomenon and not necessarily worse in a racially mixed marriage. In contrast, Ramatoulaye is shown to be understanding and helpful in her children's relationships.

In other cases, women are shown to be victims, not of their mother-in-law, but of their own mother. Binetou does not want to marry the older Modou, but her mother sees the union as the means of escaping poverty and wears her daughter down with tears and supplications. Ramatoulaye and Daba blame "Lady Mother-in-law" more than the girl. As Daba says, Binetou is "un agneau immolé comme beaucoup d'autres sur l'autel du 'matériel'" (60) [a lamb slaughtered on the altar of affluence (39)]. After the wedding, Binetou takes her revenge by becoming Modou's oppressor. She prevents him from seeing his first family by having hysterics whenever he suggests it. Yet she is still the loser, not only because of Modou's age. Afraid of the influence of her peers, he removes her from high school just as she is about to graduate in return for a monthly payment to her mother. After Modou's death, when his mother-in-law tries to hold on to her material gains, Daba says to her:

Comment une femme peut-elle saper le bonheur d'une autre femme? Tu ne
mérites aucune pitié. Déménage. Quant à Binetou, c'est une victime, ta victime.
Je la plains (103).

How can a woman sap the happiness of another? You deserve no pity. Pack up.
As for Binetou, she is a victim, your victim. I feel sorry for her (71).

The greed of Binetou's mother has destroyed the happiness of two
women. Binetou remains aloof from the struggle over the inheritance:
"Elle était déjà morte intérieurement ... depuis ses épousailles avec
Modou" (103) [She was already dead inside ... ever since her marriage
to Modou (73)]. Young Nabou is even more of a puppet in the hands of
her aunt, as she is unaware of the secret plans for her future. A
traditional village girl, she simply obeys. Tante Nabou decides
everything for her, choosing her profession of midwife. The young
woman is content with both her career and her husband, so, although
others may see her as a victim, she is not clearly defined as one in the
novel. She belongs to a social system that has largely disappeared from
urban life. As such, her portrait stands in contrast to that of the young
city women, Binetou and Daba.

In *Un Chant écarlate*, there is no parallel character to either Binetou
or Young Nabou. Ouleymatou initiates the relationship with Ousmane,
and then her family members encourage it for their own financial gain.
Ouleymatou is not presented sympathetically. She rejects the adolescent
Ousmane because he helps his mother with the housework and it is only
when she sees that he has become a desirable match that she supposedly
falls in love. Ambition appears to be the main stimulus. She is totally
unconcerned about any unhappiness she might cause Mireille, probably
because Mireille is white, but also because Ouleymatou comes from a
polygamous family and a poor environment where individuals look after
themselves unless group interests are threatened. There is no generation
conflict in her family and she is helped by her mother and her father's
first wife, Mère Fatim. The latter is regarded in her community as a

pillar of virtue and the upholder of a strict moral code, but when she sees that the whole family will benefit from a union between Ouleymatou and Ousmane, she encourages it even before marriage. Some women in Bâ's novels are prepared to destroy others' happiness to further their own aims. By no means are her female characters all depicted in a positive light.

Yet all the men, of Bâ's generation at least, are presented negatively in their principal role, which is that of husband, whatever they may be like in their professional life. With respect to his career, Modou appears to have more ambition than integrity, but Mawdo gives himself tirelessly to his work as a physician, as does the doctor who treats Jacqueline. Daouda Deng, Ramatoulaye's suitor, is said to be honorable both in his marriage and as a politician, but he too is prepared to take his life-long love as a second wife, thereby entering into a polygamous marriage. It seems that Bâ excuses him because he has always loved Ramatoulaye and only married his cousin through a sense of duty and not for love. In *Un Chant écarlate*, Ousmane's father is superficially a positive figure. In reality, he is a weak man, closing his eyes to wrong-doing to avoid conflict. Like many old men in African novels, he is more concerned with the next life than with this one.

Social Criticism

In her exposure of African values with regard to marriage and relationships between men and women, Bâ reveals flaws in Senegalese society that are closely related to the transition from traditional to modern ways. The old ideas about caste and marriage, including polygamy, are presented as the survival of an anachronistic mentality out of place in modern urban life. The distinction between people based on caste may be accepted in Tante Nabou's village, but for modern Senegalese women like Ramatoulaye and Aïssatou equality of education and convergence of views are much more important as a basis for marriage. Although the main theme of Bâ's novels is the failure of marriage, she is not against it as such, as some western feminists are.

What she rejects is the common situation in African marriages (described by Ramatoulaye in chapter 2) where a wife gives up her personality and her dignity, becoming what she calls a thing in the service of a man. Bâ says that although she is divorced, she hopes to marry again. Ramatoulaye makes the same claim to Aïssatou, telling her that she understands her friend's desire to be independent, but she herself cannot conceive of happiness outside the couple (ch. 17). She desperately hopes for a suitable partner to replace Modou, but not just anyone. In a scene paralleling the announcement of Modou's second marriage, a delegation declares the readiness of his elder brother to accept her as fourth wife after the period of mourning. Ramatoulaye at last revolts against the role she has been taught to play: "Ma voix connaît trente années de silence, trente années de brimades. Elle éclate, violente, tantôt sarcastique, tantôt méprisante" (85). [My voice has known thirty years of silence, thirty years of harassment. It bursts out, violent sometimes sarcastic, sometimes contemptuous (58)]. She refuses to be just another source of revenues for a man whose indolence his present wives struggle to support. The opinion of commentators is divided about whether Ramatoulaye is progressive or not. Some criticize her for being a creature of compromise. Florence Stratton sees her as a woman who has condemned herself to a living death on the sacrificial altar of marriage and motherhood. This is not the point of view of the novel. Aïssatou and Ramatoulaye represent two different but valid ways of reacting. Because of the deep sympathy Bâ creates for her narrator, she evidently does not see her story as one of failure and that of her friend as a success. Aïssatou chooses to leave Senegal to establish a new life. Outside the confines of the text, it could be added that the problems of love, sex and family are complex and individual in every society. Bâ shows that each woman must find her own solution through reflection.

Bâ's main crusade is against polygamy. She says to Harrell-Bond that taking a second wife merely makes it easier for a man to take a third or a fourth, but increasing the number of wives does not solve the fundamental problems between men and women. She describes Modou's monogamous relationship with Ramatoulaye as an ideal one. Before his second marriage he is an example of an enlightened man. From the Harrell-Bond interview it is clear that Ramatoulaye and Aïssatou also represent Bâ's opinion when they refuse to recognize the distinction often made by men between love and the sexual act. Both female protagonists in *Une Si Longue Lettre* see polygamy as a moral and material betrayal and denounce it outright. Yet in her refusal of Daouda Dieng, Ramatoulaye's attitude is not so categorical. Although she mentions his wife as a major reason for her rejection of his suit, in both her thoughts and her letter to him, she only does so *after* she has admitted that she does not love him. She even exclaims, just after saying that her heart says no: "Comme j'aurais voulu être mobilisée pour cet homme et pouvoir dire oui!" (97) [How I should have liked to be galvanized in favour of this man, to be able to say yes! (66)]. Does this mean when she is not personally involved that she is not so critical of polygamy? Nor is Daouda Deng condemned for wanting to take a second wife, because he has always loved Ramatoulaye. Bâ was not ambivalent in her statements about polygamy, but her narrator is at least unconsciously so.

In *Un Chant écarlate*, Ousmane is not from a polygamous family. When he witnesses the neighbors' problems, he is grateful to his father for not marrying again. Next door, Mère Fatim is an ogress who victimizes her co-wives, creating conflicts that lead to their repudiation. Another character, Tante Kiné, has a harrowing life as third wife. Yet these examples are marginal compared to the dilemma of Mireille, who, once she knows about Ouleymatou, must opt to stay or to go. Her vacillation between the two alternatives is part of the aforementioned debate about men's desire conducted by an objective voice, the clinical tone of which indicates a professional opinion disguised as Mireille's thoughts (III,10). Various arguments are presented, particularly in reference to the situation of children, but they result in nothing conclusive about what a woman should do. Bâ once again appears to be saying that each woman should make up her own mind. Mireille decides to stay, because she loves Ousmane and because she has burnt her

bridges in France. Her decision is identical to that of Ramatoulaye. At
the end of the novel it proves fatal, but the reader is sympathetic to her
reasons for making it. Both novels show that polygamy crushes a
woman's dignity and self-respect. Ramatoulaye deals with the problem
by relying on friendship. Mireille as a foreigner, although supported by
Ousmane's sister, does not succeed in conquering the alienation that
finally destroys her.

Another component of Senegalese society questioned by Bâ,
particularly through the predicament of Ramatoulaye, is Islam. Ella
Brown believes there is a deliberately orchestrated contrast between the
religious faith of the narrator and her sufferings, which are related to
practices sanctioned by Islam, such as polygamy. In Brown's opinion, Bâ
has found a discreet means of protest more effective with her compatriots
than direct attack. Bâ's attitude to Islam is certainly ambivalent. She
censures the hypocritical use of religion as an instrument of male
domination, especially with the connivance of the official representative,
the Imam. The will of God is the justification for Modou's second
marriage, but he ignores the requirement that the first wife be informed
in advance and subsequently disobeys the Islamic command to treat both
wives the same. Ousmane's behavior is almost identical. He claims to be
a good Muslim and uses Mireille's conversion to vindicate his polygamy,
but he never informs her. At the very end of *Une Si Longue Lettre* Bâ
mentions religion along with unjust legislation as having sealed the fate
of women. The official hierarchies of many religions (Bâ was certainly
not referring exclusively to Islam) have used religion as a medium of
oppression. Yet Bâ advocates genuine religious faith and practice. In *Un
Chant écarlate* Ali warns Ousmane that he has strayed away from the
religious virtues he grew up with and that his treatment of Mireille is
inviting the wrath of God (III,6). If one takes Ali to be the voice of
reason and perhaps of Bâ, there is a clear distinction in her mind
between truly following the precepts of Islam and using it as a means of
control, particularly of women.

Mariama Bâ's attitude to tradition and progress is not simplistic. She understands the complexity of the situation and does not fall into the categorical approach that rejects tradition and welcomes progress. She shows in *Un Chant écarlate* that the problem of identity is a genuine one for Africans like Ousmane who receive a western-style education. Ousmane's crime is not that he chooses to be African, but that he does it after marrying a European and then uses his identity crisis as an excuse. Some aspects of modern Senegal are profoundly disturbing to Bâ. Ramatoulaye can be taken as her mouthpiece when she condemns the power of money, which appears to be the sole criterion for status in the new urban society. Mère Fatim is supposed to be virtue itself, but when Ousmane has sexual relations with Ouleymatou before marriage, her conscience is quickly stifled by money. The exaggerated exhibitionism at Modou's funeral, where astonishing quantities of banknotes change hands, reminds Ramatoulaye of all the people whose illnesses could have been cured by the money spent at their funerals. Ostensibly money is given freely and without a thought, but in reality everything is written down and becomes a debt to be repaid at a later date.

Ramatoulaye is also worried about the influence on her daughters of some modern customs. She accepts trousers, but she balks at smoking and is shocked when her second daughter becomes pregnant before marriage. By no means does Bâ advocate a whole-hearted espousal of change for its own sake. In *Une Si Longue Lettre* her narrator looks for a reconciliation between the old and the new involving a critical examination of each in order to create a better society.

Towards a Better Society

Whatever others may say about the freedom of African women, Bâ clearly believes that it is too limited, like that of women everywhere. In her acceptance speech for the Noma award, she said that she wanted to serve as an inspiration to all women to help what she called "our common liberation" (Harrell-Bond 2). Her desire for change is passionately and poetically expressed in the last chapter of *Une Si Longue Lettre*:

Mon coeur est en fête chaque fois qu'une femme émerge de l'ombre. Je sais mouvant le terrain des acquis, difficile la survie des conquêtes: les contraintes sociales bousculent toujours et l'égoïsme mâle résiste (129).

My heart rejoices each time a woman emerges from the shadows. I know that the field of our gains is unstable, the retention of conquests difficult: social constraints are ever present, and male egoism resists (88).

Bâ does not present categorical solutions. She offers possibilities that could create a more harmonious society and heal the rift between the sexes. One of these possibilities is a change in mentality on the part of both men and women with regard to their relationship. Bâ discloses her hope in the new generation by showing us some young couples whose involvement with each other is more intimate and more egalitarian than that of their elders. Ramatoulaye's daughter Daba rejects the idea of a marriage controlled by the husband, be it polygamous or monogamous. She sees marriage as a voluntary union to be dissolved by either party if it ceases to be satisfying. Her husband Abou declares that a wife is not a slave or a servant (ch. 22). The second daughter, Aïssatou, is still at school when she becomes pregnant, so she and her boyfriend decide not to marry immediately. He is an honorable partner, respectful towards his future wife and determined to support her scholastic success. Daba and Aïssatou consider their mother's acceptance of polygamy wrong and Daba in particular harshly condemns her father.

Although in *Un Chant écarlate* Ousmane blames the failure of his marriage on racial and cultural differences, the possibility of a harmonious relationship in which both partners retain their identity is presented in a discussion of racially mixed marriages (III, 4). It is said there are cases where both man and wife feel free to follow their own customs without tension or conflict and the children are at ease in both worlds. There is, however, no example of such a situation in the book, although the young Senegalese Muslim couple, Rosalie and Ali, appear to have an enlightened marriage by Bâ's standards. Thus happy couples exist in both novels. Yet Ramatoulaye's and Aïssatou's marriages began well. One therefore wonders how these new relationships will develop and whether these progressive young men will later become polygamists.

The couple is of prime importance in the struggle for a society in which men and women work together, but when that partnership does not function satisfactorily and impedes the advancement of women, female solidarity is essential. In this respect the younger generation may become the moral arbiters for their parents. Ousmane's sister befriends Mireille and tries to help her adapt, attacking her mother's vicious behavior by pointing out that Mireille is somebody's daughter too (III, 9). Rosalie criticizes Ouleymatou on the same grounds: "Son attitude est indigne de la femme de ce siècle. Les femmes doivent être solidaires" (205) [Her attitude is unworthy of a modern woman. Women should stick together (136)]. Ramatoulaye is Bâ's principal representative as an advocate for female solidarity and her friendship with Aïssatou is the strongest example of mutual dependence. She is also the character most committed to the common cause of women everywhere. In the Harrell-Bond interview, however, Bâ claims that African women are different from western women in that they are more confident about their femininity and do not want to imitate men. Nevertheless they want basic liberties that have nothing to do with fundamental sex roles. When Ramatoulaye is abandoned by Modou and suddenly finds herself obliged to do everything alone, she discovers she is sometimes an object of curiosity, at the cinema, for example. She realizes how little freedom of movement women have in her society because of prejudice. In public life, she admits in her conversation with Daouda Dieng, women have made important gains in the fields of education and employment, but she complains that it is almost impossible for women to enter the political sphere. Yet through Daba, Bâ seems to be saying that women gain by not engaging in party politics, a corrupt expression of the male desire for personal power. Daba calls for greater participation by women at the level of local women's organizations because they are more democratic and more effective. Bâ herself was active in a women's organization called Soeurs Optimistes Internationales.

Bâ also has great faith in education and in the power of books as
"tools, instruments for development", as she expressed it in her
acceptance speech for the Noma award. On the same occasion she also
said: "People must be cultured, instructed and educated, so that things
can advance" (Harrell-Bond 3). Ramatoulaye talks of herself and her
fellow student teachers as "de véritables soeurs destinées à la même
mission émancipatrice". (27) [true sisters, destined for the same mission
of emancipation (15)]. Later, when they enter the profession, she
describes their work in military terms. The teachers are a noble army,
whose exploits go largely unrecognized, but who nonetheless plant the
flag of knowledge and virtue wherever they go. Ramatoulaye is equally
lyrical when she describes the function of books, to which she attributes
the salvation of Aïssatou: "Instrument unique de relation et de culture,
moyen inégalé de donner et de recevoir" (51) [Sole instrument of
interrelationships and of culture, unparalleled means of giving and
receiving (32)[10]]. There is no anguish in Bâ about the colonial education
system, bequeathed almost intact to independent Senegal. She sees it as
the road to consciousness and therefore to freedom.

To sum up, when Mariama Bâ's ideas about the duty of the African
woman writer are compared with the form and content of her novels, it
is evident that she lived up to her own standards. She combines a
commitment to feminism with a desire to create works of art and not
political or social pamphlets, although occasionally her didacticism is too
direct. When *Une Si Longue Lettre* first appeared, some critics were
scathing about its literary merit. In a 1982 book review, F. I. Case (who
had only read the English translation) even went so far as to question the
publication policies of Les Nouvelles Editions Africaines and Heinemann,
as well as the criteria used for judging texts for the Noma award. More
than a decade later, both Mariama Bâ's novels are generally considered
a worthy contribution to African and world literature, although the first
remains the undisputed favorite. Some critics complain that Bâ's
viewpoint is essentially aristocratic. This may be true in *Une Si Longue*

Lettre because of the social class and personal situation of the narrator. In *Un Chant écarlate*, however, she is sympathetic to the hardships of poverty and sensitive to a social structure where marriage is sometimes the only means of escaping to a better life.

It is perhaps in the last chapter of *Une Si Longue Lettre* that Bâ communicates her essential message, which does not change in her second novel, despite its pessimistic ending. The nation is founded on the family and the family is founded on the couple and the couple is founded on love. Bâ is certainly a feminist, but she does not hate men. She ties her hopes for the future of her country to a genuine partnership between men and women, based on a true understanding of their common cultural heritage and faith in religion. Her interests are not confined, however, to her own country, nor even to her own continent. Indeed, a few pages earlier in the novel she stresses that she believes in unity between all peoples: "Les mêmes remèdes soignent les mêmes maux sous tous les cieux, que l'individu soit noir ou blanc: tout unit les hommes" (116) [The same remedies cure the same illnesses everywhere under the sun, whether the individual be white or black. Everything unites men (79)]. Her final word in the Harrell-Bond interview is: "Men must love and help each other." Even if her second novel reveals the difficulty of that task, it clearly remained Mariama Bâ's most cherished ideal.

IV

Aminata Sow Fall

Aminata Sow Fall began publishing just after Diallo and before Bâ, but her work was not widely acknowledged until the appearance of her second novel in the same year as Bâ's first. Because of both the quantity and quality of her literary output, she is now considered the most important living woman novelist from francophone Black Africa. To date she has published five novels: *Le Revenant* (1976), *La Grève des Bàttu* (1979), *L'Appel des arènes* (1982), *L'Ex-père de la nation* (1987) and *Le Jujubier du patriarche* (1993). Her second novel was shortlisted for the Prix Goncourt in 1979 and won the Grand Prix Littéraire de l'Afrique Noire in 1981.

Unlike Bâ and Nafissatou Diallo, Sow Fall has written nothing even vaguely autobiographical. All her protagonists are male and all but one of her novels are written in the third person with multiple viewpoints. Furthermore, Sow Fall stresses in her numerous interviews that she is not a feminist novelist. She recognizes that subjects such as polygamy may be treated more convincingly by women, but claims that she writes as a citizen, not specifically as a woman. This preoccupation with general social trends is clearly reflected in Sow Fall's writing. Each novel aims to expose an aspect of Senegalese society that touches everyone. The content and form of her books recall those of her compatriot, Sembène Ousmane, whose work deals with the plight of ordinary men and women in modern, capitalist, urban society. In a 1984 interview with Milolo Kembe, Sow Fall explains that on her return to Africa after seven years in France, she was astonished by the changes in Senegalese society and decided to write about the new reality (294). In a 1981 interview with Thomas Hammond, she highlights the social relevance of the novel form. Although previously attracted to other genres, she chose the novel as the best medium of expression for her ideas (192).

Sow Fall's novels together create a comprehensive picture of modern Senegal. Each concentrates on one social problem, represented by a powerful symbol that is truly African. *Le Revenant* is about the role of money in urban life. More subtly, it is also about the hypocrisy which pervades society and dictates behavior and relationships. This hypocrisy finds its most potent symbol in *xeesal*. In *La Vie quotidienne en Afrique Noire à travers la littérature africaine* Patrick Mérand comments on the recent proliferation of *xeesal* in the form of a wide variety of pastes and powders for lightening the skin (103). Not only do the women in the novel use *xeesal*, but it also indispensable for the protagonist's faked return from the dead.

The main theme of *La Grève des Bàttu* is the interdependence of all members of society and the necessary correlation between giving and receiving. The central symbol is the "bàttu" or begging bowl. Although widespread conversions to Islam did not take place in Senegal until the nineteenth century, some regions were Muslim by the eleventh century, and it is generally perceived as an authentically African religion. *Zakat*, the giving of alms at particular times in the religious calendar, is one of the Five Pillars of Islam and *Sadakat*, the casual daily giving, is highly recommended. The Prophet says: 'The hand that gives is better (with Allah) than the hand that takes.'[11] Boys often spend part of their childhood as *talibés*, or apprentices to a holy-man and have to beg for their food. Charity is also considered a vital means of gaining divine favor to assure the desired outcome to a particular situation. People give in order to receive. When the beggars go on strike, the social equilibrium is destroyed.

In the conflict between tradition and westernization exposed in *L'Appel des arènes*, the wrestling arena is the symbol of all that is positive in traditional life. In Mérand's book, wrestling is the only African sport mentioned (139) and Daryll Gamble describes it as "the favorite sport of all the Senegalese peoples" (77). African wrestling is not merely a sport. It is a complete cultural experience, recreating the historic role of the warrior in a spectacle of music, song, and dance.

Sow Fall's fourth novel, *L'Ex-père de la nation,* is a meditation on power in the newly independent African nations. The central symbol is the sun, Africa being referred to as "les pays du soleil" (165) [the lands of the sun]. The sinister foreign advisor, Andru, says that African rulers must control their people like the sun, offering them the illusion of happiness combined with oppression (167). During the presidency of Madiama, the sun becomes an even greater instrument of oppression because of the terrible drought. As he sets out to write his memoirs (the novel itself) Madiama meditates on the appropriateness of the sun as a symbol for power. He realizes that he too has been dazzled by illusion. The sun returns in all its glory with each new day, but his power has declined for ever.

In *Le Jujubier du patriarche* the central symbol is the tree of the title. Growing out of the tomb of the noble ancestor of seven hundred years ago, it used to give miraculous fruit; but ravaged by the attentions of the pilgrims it eventually died. One day it bursts into life again. Together with the never-ending epic chant about the heroic deeds of the ancestors, it symbolizes the necessity for the life-giving renaissance of tradition in modern African life.

Tradition and Progress

These powerful African symbols relate to the main underlying theme of Sow Fall's writing, cultural conflict. They all represent traditional cyclical time as opposed to the linear nature of progress. *Xeesal* is associated in *Le Revenant* with the return of the dead to life, as is the tree of the patriarch. The begging bowl, the wrestling arena and the sun are circular in form and could be seen as the expression of an ever-recurring ritual or cycle.

Cultural conflict is revealed through three fundamental but overlapping oppositions: the change between the past and the present, the contrast between the village and the city and the all-encompassing clash between traditional Africa and the West. As Sow Fall says in a 1975 article written with Rose Senghor, the fundamental question for modern Africans is which traditions to keep and which to reject. In her novels, she suggests some answers to this question. She wrote *Le Revenant* because she was shocked by the negative changes which had occurred in Senegal during her seven-year absence. The attitude of her protagonist, Bakar, after his release from prison, reflects this reaction, "Le monde d'aujourd'hui est bouleversé" (87) [Today's world is turned upside down[12]]. He feels lost in a society more attached to money than to the dignity of the individual.

The relationship between the past and the present is not directly treated in *La Grève des Bàttu*, but *L'Appel des arènes* constantly evokes a past which continues to exist through the consciousness of the wrestlers, André and Malaw. This spiritual cultural heritage is communicated through folk-stories, legends, and genealogy, all stressing virtues such as courage, honor and dignity. In traditional African life, the relationship with one's ancestors is at the core of the individual's identity. When the boy Nalla makes the acquaintance of André and Malaw, he enters a magic world, full of riddles, symbols, and mysteries (113), a world in which past and present are united. André tells him about his family's pact with their totem, the snake, since time immemorial (38) and describes his friendship with Malaw as part of a relationship between families over many generations (45). Listening to Malaw remember his father, reputed to be half-man, half-lion, Nalla laments the disappearance of so many wonderful things. Malaw replies: "Parce que *Cosaan* se meurt, mon petit" (95) [Because tradition is dying, little one]. Through Malaw, Nalla discovers the sacred baobab tree, the symbol of life. By nourishing itself from the ground in which the ancestors lie, it creates a link between them and their descendants. Nalla's parents have rejected traditional Africa as barbaric, but the boy finds the life and values they offer him cold and sterile. He turns instead to the enchantment and communal warmth of the wrestling arena.

L'Ex-père de la nation is an attempt by the imprisoned narrator, Madiama, to understand his life, in particular his accession to the presidency and subsequent fall from power. Inserted into his account of the last eight years is a series of flashbacks, revealing not only Madiama's own past, but also what he knows of the origins of his parents. There is no evocation of an idyllic existence as in *L'Appel des arènes*, but the cumulative impression is of a world of clear and positive values, represented still by his half-brother, Bara.

In *Le Jujubier du patriarche*, past and present are woven together, spanning the centuries between the lives of the heroes in the epic chant and those of their modern-day descendants. Once again, the beginning of the text is chronologically the end. As the narrative progresses, a picture slowly emerges of the two sets of lives, completed in the twenty-page excerpt from the chant that closes the novel. At first the distant past is presented as a hindrance. Yelli is prevented from coming to terms with reality by his consciousness of his noble origins. The epic chant is also a source of dissension. It validates the perpetuation of the caste system in the minds of the characters, especially of Yelli's wife, Tacko. Finally, however, the past becomes a means of reconciliation and rebirth. The communal spirit is rekindled and peace and harmony reestablished.

Although rapid change is occurring everywhere in Africa, traditional life survives to some extent in the village. Yet accelerated urbanization is causing many Senegalese to lose contact with their rural origins. Even if the old values persist in the city, particularly in the poor districts, they do not have the same moral power. The main action of Sow Fall's novels takes place in the city, but the village is always a significant presence. *Le Revenant* is set in Dakar, but Bakar is befriended by Hélène, a young woman who left her village to look for work. She is the only person to help him unselfishly, apart from his mother and old friend, Sada. The first time Bakar meets her, he is astonished by her open and friendly manner, indicative of the courtesy and hospitality toward strangers in the country. Hélène represents natural goodness, in sharp contrast to the corruption of human relationships in Dakar.

In *La Grève des Bàttu*, the values of Serigne Birama, the rural holy-man or *marabout*, contrast with those of the ruthlessly progressive politicians, Mour and Kéba. When Mour first makes the acquaintance of the *marabout*, he remarks that the moral plenitude of the villager seems to belong to another world (12). On discovering that Mour is clearing the streets of beggars to help the tourist industry, Serigne Birama exclaims: "La Ville est en train de vous déshumaniser, d'endurcir vos coeurs." (26) [The City is dehumanising you, hardening people's hearts]. Dakar, never mentioned by name, is always referred to as "la Ville", further underlining the intended opposition between the city and the country. Only in the city are the beggars seen as a scourge. One of their leaders, Ngirane, tells his companions that, despite the poverty of his village, the more fortunate instinctively shared with those in need (83). In the city, human beings are merely statistics and the poor areas are described as "zones malsaines" (91) [unhealthy zones] to be destroyed in the name of progress, without any thought for the people.

The moral and spiritual superiority of village life is made even clearer in *L'Appel des arènes*. Nalla spends part of his childhood in the country with his grandmother, Mame Fari, where he lives in harmony with nature and people, surrounded by love. Later, he rediscovers this lost paradise with André, who takes the boy on a journey of the imagination to his beautiful Saalum. Malaw's native village, Diaminar, is also endowed with a mythical power and evoked with the same lyricism. Like the Saalum, it symbolizes mystery and love as well as peace and unity between man and nature. Slowly, however, Diaminar loses its population to the city. Malaw's father sees ten of his children leave, including his daughter, who dies in prison after murdering her illegitimate baby. In an apocalyptic speech, he warns Malaw of the dangers of city life. It deadens the souls of its inhabitants, turning them into brutes or madmen who destroy each other (128). He begs Malaw to save humanity by going to the town of Louga and establishing a wrestling arena, from which the tam-tam will call mankind back to the ancestral earth. Shortly afterwards, Malaw's father dies and Diaminar is abandoned, but the village lives on in the hearts of its people and in the praise poems to the great wrestler, Malaw Lô.

Madiama in *L'Ex-père de la nation* grew up in a coastal village. It not only represents the innocence of his childhood, but also surviving moral rectitude through the father-figure of his older brother, Bara, a retired fisherman. Madiama sees Bara as his conscience and throughout his life he draws on the moral strength and vision of the older man. When Madiama becomes alienated from the people, he cannot face his brother. Like Serigne Birama, Bara lives in a spiritually superior world, uncorrupted by city values.

In *Le Jujubier du patriarche* the ancestor's tomb is in a small village in the remote Foudjallon. When the descendants of the epic heroes decide to return to their origins, the journey turns into an annual pilgrimage, resuscitating both the village and the visitors. It is no longer enough to keep the village alive in one's memories. They can become distorted so far from the source. The city now has to return to the village for spiritual renewal and inner peace.

Sow Fall sometimes presents the antagonism between traditions and modernity as a conflict between the western and the African way. Although *Le Revenant* makes no direct reference to the West, the most important symbol of hypocrisy is *xeesal.* The *xeesal* merchant makes the association overtly by claiming that his product can give a Senegalese the complexion of a European within a week (104). Thus, attachment to appearances, portrayed as an integral part of the increasing materialism, is represented by a symbol that relates it to the West. In this way, Sow Fall subtly unites the psychological and the material aspects of westernization.

In *La Grève des Bàttu* she is more explicit. The new leaders of Senegal are trying to rule the country according to western norms. The beggars are said to threaten public hygiene and the national economy (7) because of the importance of tourism (26). The reference to tourism serves to emphasize that the attitude of the leaders to the beggars is foreign to Senegal. The ordinary people do not understand the desire of the authorities to eliminate a group that has always had its rightful place in society. This divergence of opinion reveals the difference in mentality between the western-oriented upper classes and the rest of the population. Ironically, what is good for tourism is not good for the country as a whole. The city can no longer function properly when the beggars retire to the outskirts of the town. The case of tourism becomes representative of foreign influence on the mentality and political decisions of African leaders. Another example of this influence is the evacuation of the poor areas. The minister responsible adopts a pseudo-scientific approach to the problem, in what is an obvious satire of those Africans attempting to imitate western rationalism. Mour finds the minister's statement ridiculous, although he himself is attracted to his second wife because of her excellent command of French.

In *L'Appel des arènes,* the conflict between western and African ways is still more explicit through the characterization of Nalla's mother, Diattou. She grew up in the communal life of the village, but goes through a metamorphosis in France, where she accompanies her husband. The village elders are shocked by her clothing and behavior on her return, but Diattou scornfully dismisses their disapproval, in the name of progress and individual liberty (122). Because of her ideas on modernity, she isolates Nalla from his grandmother and the neighborhood community, leading to a general boycott of the family. After the death of a little boy she banned from the house, Diattou is branded a witch, a "mangeuse d'âme", and the family is forced to move. Yet she continues to see herself as a civilized person among the barbarians. She has all the stereotypical prejudices associated with white racism towards blacks. Nalla does not experience "la case de l'homme," traditional circumcision so important in Africa in the accession to manhood. His grandmother had talked of it for years, but Diattou has no tolerance for what she calls a simple medical act. She has cut off her roots completely. Although her husband shares many of her opinions, their conception of society is fundamentally different. Ndiogou is of noble blood but no longer believes in the old divisions. In contrast, Diattou sees westernization as the means of creating a new hierarchy with herself at the top. At the end of the novel, no one attends her maternity clinic because of her reputation as a "mangeuse d'âme". She has become a tragic figure, an embodiment of cultural conflict in its most destructive form.

The strongest criticism of western influence appears in *L'Ex-père de la nation*. Neither the African country nor the former colonial power is named, emphasizing the common destiny of the continent. The country is controlled by "the North", or "the Metropolis" or "our Northern partners." The foreign power, represented by Andru, puts Madiama into the presidency, keeps him there despite general opposition and deposes him when he no longer serves their purpose. The interests of the West are contrary to the good of the African people and Independence is a farce.

In *Le Jujubier du patriarche* there seems to be a deliberate attempt to create an exclusively African context. Near the beginning, however, the expulsion from Zaire of 1200 Africans from neighboring countries leads to a conversation among the victims in which whites and African leaders are criticized in the same vein as in *L'Ex-père de la nation*. Bitter mention is also made of the sordid racism in Europe, the only reward for African sacrifices in the War (21). The rest of the novel ignores outside influences to concentrate on the need for Africans to find African solutions to their alienation.

Two related themes, integral elements in the clash between the old and the new, cut across the distinctions in time and place examined above. The first is the interdependence of all members of the community, treated most obviously in *La Grève des Bàttu* but central to all of Sow Fall's work. The second is a questioning about what it means to be a human being. The most fundamental difference between traditional

Africa and modern western life lies in the relationship between the community and the individual. In Africa, the community is of primary importance, and to remain part of it, one must accept its norms. In return, it cares for its members and gives them spiritual and cultural identity. Nevertheless, communal values are weakening, particularly in the cities, and what was referred to as western individualism is now also becoming an African phenomenon.

The breakdown of communal values has not yet occurred in *Le Revenant*. Society is still based on exchange and interdependence, but in a corrupted form. Money is the principal means to power and virtue alone no longer counts: "Les pauvres ne méritent aucun intérêt, fussent-ils nantis des meilleures qualités humaines" (39) [The poor deserve no consideration, even when they possess the greatest human virtues]. Generosity opens all doors and no questions are asked about the source of wealth by the beneficiaries. Yama, Bakar's beautiful and intelligent sister, understands at an early age the new forces which govern society: "Avec le bouleversement des structures sociales, une puissance nouvelle avait été créée . . . Des principes aussi durs que l'acier pouvaient être réduits à néant, et des murailles naguère interdites et infranchissables pouvaient être enjambées au nom de cet idéal matériel qu'on faisait semblant de mépriser." (34) [With the overturning of social structures, a new power had been created . . . Principles as hard as steel could be reduced to nothing and previously forbidden and unscaleable walls could be stepped over in the name of this material ideal that people pretended to despise]. Communal values are no longer the reason for giving. As Bâ too points out, money given is really money lent and debts must be repaid twice-over at a later date. At the same time, "generosity" is accorded enormous respect, so that money apparently distributed with abandon is in fact a powerful means to social prestige and advancement. This relationship is revealed transparently when Yama, still poor and unmarried, dances at a public celebration. Her casual attitude to the money showered on her is an important factor in her marriage to a rich man five months later. She uses his money to establish herself as a *diriyanké,* or society hostess, and becomes famous for the lavishness of her hospitality. Her extravagance is part of a calculated plan to acquire power, illustrated in detail at the baptism of Bakar's baby daughter. The occasion turns into a competition between Yama and Bakar's in-laws, similar to that in Diallo's *La Princesse de Tiali.* To lose means public shame. Yama is prepared to spend a fortune and therefore wins.

Marriage, too, is presented as an investment to which poverty is an obstacle. Yama's husband is so rich that he can afford to choose her for her beauty and talents, but she needs his money to make Bakar's love-match possible. When Bakar heaps gifts on his wife and her family, as well as on his own family, nobody bothers to ask where the money comes from, although his modest salary alone could never permit such generosity. Yet on his conviction and imprisonment, he is immediately abandoned by those he helped. Forced to give his wife a divorce, Bakar finds himself a total outcast, without a job and with only his mother and friend, Sada.

Seduced by the values prevalent in his community, Bakar had fallen victim to the attitude that the end is more important than the means. Wrongdoing is sanctioned as long as it is hidden. In a society addicted to appearances, public exposure of crime entails loss of dignity and the community protects itself by rejecting the individual. The interdependence of the different members of the group is still a reality, but the values sustaining and motivating the group are corrupt. This degeneration of the communal spirit is shown through the theme of the "bulletin nécrologique," the death announcements on the radio accompanied by a list of mourners. The prison inmates listen to them eagerly, as if the solidarity displayed brought them closer to the outside world. Yet, as with the family celebrations, this solidarity is an illusion. The death notices are an opportunity for living individuals to put themselves, not the deceased, into the lime-light. Ironically, those who compose the lists of mourners are often so preoccupied with their own social prestige that they forget to name the deceased. Yama's list for Bakar includes every person of importance in Dakar. As Yama ignored her brother's existence after his conviction, the extent of the hypocrisy of the funeral broadcasts becomes clear. The list is really an advertisement of Yama's social contacts and influence, real or desired, and has nothing to do with Bakar's death. His death notice takes up the whole of the thirty minutes allotted to the morning news, and has to be continued at a later time. Ostensibly an expression of grief at the death of a member of the community, the death notices are one more illustration of Sow Fall's view of the hollowness of human relationships in modern city life.

La Grève des Bàttu develops the idea of exchange in a new way. Whereas in the preceding novel the poor are disenfranchised, in her second novel Sow Fall reveals that the beggars, apparently most dependent on others, are in reality as influential as anyone else, because charity is a necessary way of seeking divine help. The holy-man, Serigne Birama, reminds Mour that he must give as often as he can, because his fortune is a divine loan, not a permanent gift (88). When the authorities try to eliminate the beggars as though they were parasites, they are confused. They have always considered themselves citizens with full rights and duties: "Pour eux le contrat qui lie chaque individu à la société se résume en ceci: donner et recevoir. Eh bien, eux, ne donnent-ils pas leurs bénédictions de pauvres, leurs prières et leurs voeux?" (30) [For them the contract that ties each individual to society can be summarized as follows: giving and receiving. Well, don't they give their blessings as poor people, their prayers and their good wishes? (83)[13]]. When the beggars withdraw from the streets, the result is chaos and the loss of work hours caused by the crowds travelling to the city outskirts is harmful to the national economy. The beggars are proven to be full members of a society whose smooth functioning is dependent on their accessible presence.

In *L'Appel des arènes,* Diattou rejects the interdependence of community living and considers the concern of the older villagers to be unwarranted interference. In response, her mother points out: "C'est notre tradition de nous regarder et de nous redresser mutuellement, ma fille" (122).[Daughter, it is our tradition to observe and correct each other]. Aware of the reciprocal relationship between rights and duties, Diattou wants neither to give nor to receive. She is unable to distinguish between base materialism and the traditional exchange, which confers dignity on both parties. This blindness leads her to call her husband's *griot* a parasite, although his visits are an expression of his ancestral allegiance to Ndiogou's family since the days of the battlefields (107). In contrast to Diattou's ideals, the wrestling arena represents giving and sharing. Malaw's father saw its establishment as a sacred social mission to save the souls of his compatriots in the face of dehumanization. Ndiogou is astonished at the end of the novel when he witnesses the racial and social diversity of the spectators, united in a joyful celebration of human strength and dignity.

In *L'Ex-père de la nation,* Madiama becomes a nurse because he wishes to devote himself to others. His father, obsessed by his own father's role as official executioner for the colonizers, sends his son to school with the promise to "laver la terre d'un peu de ses souillures" (95) [wash the world clean of some of its dirt]. Madiama never forgets his commitment. Because of his attempts to eliminate corruption in the medical profession, he spends six months in prison. Even when he becomes president, his principal motivation is the desire to help his people. Madiama truly wishes to be a father to the nation. Yet the realities of power cut him off from the community and his final incarceration is merely the concrete expression of the role of president.

Le Jujubier du patriarche is based on a complex genealogical web, slowly unravelled as the text progresses. All the main characters are descendants of the heroes of the Foudjallon epic chant, but the reversal in fortunes of the former nobles and slaves creates ill-feeling. The poverty of the modern patriarch, Yelli, contrasts with the wealth of his adopted daughter, Naarou, of slave origins. When Yelli's wife, Tacko, calls Naarou a slave at a public gathering, the clan breaks up. Only with the news of the end of the drought and the buds on the patriarch's tree is Yelli inspired to organize a pilgrimage to Babyselli. The enormous response indicates the thirst for spiritual renewal both inside and outside the clan and there is a scene of reconciliation at the patriarch's tomb. The last third of the novel that follows tells the full story of the epic, the missing links revealing the interdependence of all members of the clan and the importance of the slaves' role. Naarou's slave ancestors, Warèle and Biti, are as much heroes of the epic as the nobles. Both women sacrificed their lives to further the quest of the noble hero, Yellimané. Thus a misunderstanding of the traditional relationships had led to the breakup of the community. Furthermore, after the death of the heroine, Dioumana, the mortal enemies come together to pray over her tomb. Reconciliation is the final message of the epic chant.

The question of communal values is linked in Sow Fall's work to the definition of a human being and to the theme of life and death. In *Le Revenant*, individuals no longer have any worth in themselves. Virtue is of no account if someone is poor and people are reduced to pawns in the struggle for money and prestige. Yet Sow Fall offers no solution. Money has corrupted the sense of community, as symbolized by the death notices, so that membership means participation in a living death. Yet to be ostracized by society also means spiritual death. Bakar feels that he no longer exists. He tells Hélène that for his father and sisters he is already dead and adds: "Peux-tu comprendre la solitude d'un homme lorsqu'il se rend compte qu'il n'accomplit aucun rôle humain?" (109) [Can you understand the solitude of a man when he realizes that he fulfills no human role?]. Long before he turns up at his own funeral disguised as a ghost, he has already become one inside (98). He sees his transformation through *xeesal* as a protest against the prevailing hypocrisy and lack of moral integrity: ". . . . je serai autre, aliéné, dépersonnalisé comme ils veulent tous être" (106) [I'll be another person, alienated, depersonalized as they all want to be].

Unlike the other characters in *Le Revenant*, Hélène's appearance totally belies her inward state. Bakar is shocked by the excessive make-up that makes her look like a circus performer (78), but she is the most natural person in the novel and the most disinterestedly caring. Hélène has remained the simple country girl, even if she has adopted what she sees as a city image. Her very lack of sophistication with regard to make-up and perfume reveals her innocence. Her role is another warning not to judge by appearances.

The prominence of the theme of humanity in *La Grève des Bàttu* can be seen in its subtitle: "ou les déchets humains" [or The Dregs of Society]. As Minh-ha Trinh points out, there is a constant interplay in the novel between the terms "hommes" [men] and "chiens" [dogs]. The beggars are anxious to underline both to themselves and to their persecutors that they are not dogs (31). Yet the police behave like mad dogs when they attack the beggars (29). It is precisely to show that they are human and that: "y a des souffrances qu'on ne doit pas infliger à un être humain" (32) [there are some forms of suffering that no one has the right to inflict on a human being (23)] that the beggars go on strike.

The same play on words can be seen in the relationship between Mour and the beggars. At the beginning he represents the official point of view, exposed in the first paragraph of the novel. The beggars are described as human obstructions, as merely shadows of men. When he needs them for the distribution of charity to further his political ambitions, however, Mour tries to persuade them to return to their usual haunts by telling them to behave like humans: "Il y a si longtemps que vous êtes tapis ici, comme si vous n'étiez pas des êtres humains." (109) [You've been huddled together here for such a long time, as if you were scarcely human (82)]. Not surprisingly, his speech is greeted with laughter. Although Mour despises the beggars and dislikes their treatment of him as an equal, he is forced to swallow his pride and pretend that all men are really equals: "Tu vois, nous sommes tous pareils, nous sommes tous de même condition car nous sommes des hommes" (113) [You see, we are all equal, we are all of the same condition, for we are all human (86)]. The beggars, in turn, despise Mour when he disclaims responsibility for their ill-treatment. Salla Niang, their leader, understands he is one of those "petits" (worthless people) prepared to go to the devil to satisfy his ambition (113). Once again there is an inversion of roles, for the leaders become "les petits" and the supposedly lowest of the low, the beggars, gain in stature because they cannot be lured onto the streets by the promise of money. There is yet another reversal of roles. Beggars are usually objects of pity, but when Mour desperately tries to convince the beggars to return to the streets, he becomes a pathetic figure and, in fact, a beggar. Normally totally indifferent to the fate of the beggars, Mour is shocked and angered by their indifference to him. Once his resentment has subsided, his own need makes him understand the interdependence of all members of the community and the essential humanity of the beggars. Mour should have empathized with the beggars from the beginning, having been imprisoned for hitting a white supervisor who thought Africans were less than dogs. Unfortunately, Mour has forgotten what it was like to be treated as less than human under the colonial system.

Mour's assistant, Kéba, is also opposed to the presence of the beggars, but his reasons are different and highly personal: "il était choqué de voir des êtres humains–si pauvres fussent-ils–porter atteinte à leur dignité en quémandant d'une manière aussi honteuse et effrontée" (7) [He was shocked to see human beings–however poor they might be–diminishing their own dignity by sponging on others in such a disgraceful, shameless fashion (2)]. He is proud of the fact that his mother raised her children alone in great hardship without ever asking for help. For Kéba the campaign against the beggars is a crusade, not because they are animals, but precisely because he recognizes them as full human beings.

In *L'Appel des arènes*, the speech by Malaw's father about the dangers of the city reveals what Sow Fall thinks about the depersonalization of modern urban life (128). Nalla's teacher, Monsieur Niang, also analyses in his notebook the modern dilemma: "Le désordre qui bouleverse le monde a pour cause l'aliénation collective . . . L'homme perd ses racines et l'homme sans racines est pareil à un arbre sans racines: il se dessèche et meurt" (67) [The chaos that is destroying the world is caused by collective alienation . . . People are losing their roots and people without roots are like a tree without roots: they wither and die]. Nalla's parents inspire these reflections. Monsieur Niang predicts physical and mental unbalance for the couple and this is exactly what happens to Diattou. The paradox he exposes, exemplified in the case of Diattou, is that a fanatical adherence to individualism leads to depersonalization because of the loss of cultural identity. Ndiogou, however, rediscovers both the joys of collective living and his relationship with his son at the end of the novel, when he finally decides to go to the wrestling match. Although at one point Niang says the problem of alienation is universal, at another point he compares Africa to the West and concludes: "Chez nous, le fond de l'homme n'est pas encore mort" (104) [Here the essence of humanity is not yet dead].

In *L'Ex-père de la nation* Madiama's motto as president is "Humanité, Justice, Vérité." He believes passionately in these ideals and tries to put them into practice, just as he tried as a nurse to express his love for mankind. Yet for those who control him they are empty words. Humanity and the realities of power are incompatible. After the death of his daughter in a demonstration, Madiama becomes a different person. He blames the people for her death and his obsession with vengeance leads to oppression. The tapestry (112) in his living room sums up the basic dilemma of life. It depicts a man on a beach staring out to sea. He is wrapped in white muslin, his hand on a bone half buried in the sand. Human beings may be visionaries, but they are handicapped by their limitations and finally by their own mortality.

In *Le Jujubier du patriarche*, Naarou sees "Le mal profond qui, depuis quelques décennies, rongeaient les coeurs, appauvrissait l'esprit et souillait l'âme." (63) [The deep evil that for several decades had been gnawing at hearts, impoverishing spirits and defiling souls]. She feels she is living in "une ère de décrépitude morale où l'humain n'avait plus de sens" (63) [an era of moral decrepitude in which the human had no meaning]. Tacko illustrates this modern alienation. Her jealousy and resentment begin to destroy her soul and her body. When she says at the tomb that she wants to live, she is rejecting spiritual death and accepting the rebirth of love.

What does it mean therefore to be human in the context of Sow Fall's novels? First, it means to treat one's fellow men as people like oneself and not as animals or pawns in the struggle to rise in society. Respect and affection should govern relationships and an individual's life should be guided by moral integrity, not self-interest. To be human also signifies keeping in touch with one's roots. Imported values cannot fully replace African ones. In *L'Appel des arènes,* the bond with the land is seen by both Monsieur Niang and Malaw's father as the means of salvation from dehumanization. To be human is also to have the power of choice. When the beggars decide to assert themselves as full citizens, they claim the right to accept or reject what is offered them. Their own self-image is transformed by the recognition that they fulfill an essential role. Between *Le Revenant* and *Le Jujubier du patriarche* Sow Fall's view of the sickness eating away at African society does not change. Both *L'Appel des arènes* and her last novel, however, offer possible solutions.

Women and Men

Despite Sow Fall's claims that she is more interested in general social problems than the female condition, women occupy a special place in her work. As Trinh points out, the position of beggars relates closely to that of women. Yet whereas traditionally beggars are integrated into society and only lose their status with urbanization and modernization, women are often traditionally oppressed and gain important freedoms with progress. The oppressed female character is common in Sow Fall's novels. Bakar's mother in *Le Revenant* is typical of the hard-working, down-trodden, devoted mother to be found almost everywhere in African literature. His father is also the typical patriarch whose word is law: "Il était intransigent et voulait régner en maître. L'abnégation totale de sa femme ne l'empêchait pas d'exercer son instinct mâle de domination" (74) [He was intransigent and wanted to be the master. The total self-effacement of his wife did not stop him exercising his male instinct for domination]. Bakar vividly remembers a scene from his childhood where his father treated his mother like a dog. The next day Bakar sees her genuflecting as usual before her lord and master (76).

Notwithstanding his scandalized reaction to his father's tyranny, Bakar grows up conscious of the superiority conferred by his sex (23), but he is a tender and loving husband. His wife, however, is controlled by her parents and elders: "Mame Aïssa était femme, il n'était donc pas question pour elle d'assumer librement ses actes. Elle était conditionnée par un milieu où toute tentative de libération était considérée comme un scandale, comme une trahison" (63) [Mame Aïssa was a woman. There was therefore no question of her taking responsibility for her own actions. She was conditioned by an environment in which any attempt to be free was seen as a scandal and a betrayal]. Forced to ask Bakar for a divorce, she is quickly given as fourth wife to a rich man.

Although Bakar's friend, Sada, is a considerate person, his wife still has to assume a subservience she does not feel. She spends every weekend in the kitchen, cooking for an endless stream of card-playing male guests, a smile hiding her deep resentment: "Elle est femme et son rôle, en tant qu'épouse, n'est-il pas de tout supporter et de ne jamais se plaindre" (17). [She is a woman and her role as wife is of course to put up with everything and never complain]. Yet the point is made that some men stay away from home because they are afraid of losing face by deferring to their wives. Men are also subjected to social pressures, making it difficult for them to escape from the stereotype of male superiority.

In *La Grève des Bàttu*, Mour's wife, Lolli, represents the submissive, traditional woman. From the country, she has been brought up to believe that her dignity is grounded in her attitude of respect and obedience towards her husband, whatever he does (39). Her parents tell her a man is not a belonging. Yet the result is that the woman herself becomes a chattel of the man. She has only duties, not rights, and like the beggars must be grateful for what she is given, without any question of choice. After the early years of neglect by Mour, Lolli believes that her relationship with her husband has developed into a genuine partnership and is devastated when he presents her with a co-wife after twenty-four years of marriage. Although aware of modern feminist militancy, she is not concerned with theoretical considerations about polygamy as much as with Mour's betrayal of her years of devotion, an attitude she shares with Bâ's protagonists. Mour remains unmoved. He sees polygamy as his right and is not interested in duties. The same can be said about his relationship with the beggars, until they deny him his request. He is equally dependent on Lolli, but she refuses to test him because of her duty to her parents. After the initial eruption of revolt, she not only stays with Mour, but desperately tries to court his favor. Mour's second wife, Sine, is far more demanding than Lolli. She refuses to be at his beck and call and when he gives her orders, she retorts: "Je suis une personne et non un bout de bois" (126) [I'm a person, not a block of wood (95)]. Yet she accepts polygamy, probably because Mour is rich and powerful.

In spite of his progressive ideas in other areas, Kéba shares the stereotypical male prejudices about women. His secretary, Sagar, is more perceptive than he is about the beggars, but when she suggests that the latter are essential in a Moslem society, he shrugs her off with a comment about the superficiality and irresponsibility of women (23).

In *L'Appel des arènes* polygamy is not even mentioned and the theme of the emancipation of women is presented differently. Diattou has the freedom in her marriage and profession Sow Fall seems to be advocating. She is not the victim of others' selfishness or prejudice, but of her own misguided convictions.

Traditional female submission in the context of polygamy is again a theme in *L'Ex-père de la nation*, but Madiama's first wife reacts differently from Lolli after her initial rage. Coura's lucid decision to remain with her husband as a mother-figure and not as a wife is an expression of her strength, independence and love: "J'éprouve une joie profonde d'exprimer mon droit à l'existence quand tout apparemment concourait à m'écraser" (59) [I feel a profound joy at being able to express my right to exist when everything apparently was conspiring to crush me]. She turns polygamy into a lasting moral victory by cleansing her heart of all bitterness, while affirming her right to choose. Madiama's second wife, Yandé, is far more of a victim in her first marriage. The transformation from an adoring, obedient wife to a diabolic figure is caused by her husband's sadism. Her revenge for his years of cruelty lead to a prison sentence and social ostracism. Although a negative presence in Madiama's life, the story of her past gives Yandé a tragic dimension.

Yelli's wife, Tacko, in *Le Jujubier du patriarche* also suffers from the string of wives her husband brings home, despite his declarations of love. After Yelli's bankruptcy, only Tacko and her bitterness remain. Their daughter, Bouri, introduces a new theme into Sow Fall's work, that of sterility. Traditionally, sterility has always been blamed on the woman, and Bouri's husband tortures her with references to her infirmity, although medical examinations indicate nothing wrong. When she dares to suggest the problem might lie with him, he divorces her. Later they have a daughter and remarry, indicating that the whole question of apportioning blame for sterility is senseless.

It would be wrong to think that men always have the upper hand in Sow Fall's novels or that women are always victims. There is a significant episode at the beginning of *Le Revenant* where Bakar politely asks a woman in a bus to rearrange her headscarf to stop it hitting his face. The resulting uproar among the passengers, presumably women, effectively silences him. The arrangement of marriages is controlled by women and Yama sets out to conquer Mame Aïssa's female relatives when she decides to support her brother's marital plans. Furthermore, a unanimous decision by a family council of older women makes Mame Aïssa's divorce inevitable.

Nor are women always paragons of virtue. Some women have a weakness for money and extravagant spending. After Bakar's imprisonment, Mame Aïssa's father blames his wife's greed for the marriage: "Vous les femmes, vous êtes des démons, des démons trop sensibles à l'argent, aux folies, à la renommée" (56) [You women are demons with regard to money and reputation]. Often confined to a role more restricted than their capabilities, without education and without a profession, women immerse themselves in trivialities. Their attachment to material benefits can lead their husbands into debt or into a never-ending struggle for money. Ironically, Mame Aïssa does not ask Bakar for anything. It is his own choice to shower her and her family with gifts.

Although all Sow Fall's protagonists are men, they are fundamentally weak and highly dependent on women. Bakar's desire to please his wife and her family and to emulate his rich and powerful sister, Yama, lead to his downfall. Yet the choice to act illegally was his own and his subsequent refusal to accept blame illuminates a basic flaw in his character. Mour can be a petty tyrant with Lolli and the beggars, but he too is mediocre and inept. At home he relies totally on Lolli. With his second wife he is powerless to impose his will. At work he does everything through his assistant, Kéba. His main psychological dependence, however, is on the *marabouts* or holy-men. Knowing that his talents are limited, he puts all his faith in the supernatural. Nalla's case is different because as a child he is automatically dependent on others. Uncertain about many aspects of life, he tries to reconcile the contradictions he witnesses in the adult world. He is strong-minded enough, however, to choose Monsieur Niang and the wrestling arena in spite of his parents' opposition, but is forced to do so secretly. Madiama is a man of good will, but too naive to understand the realities of power until it is too late. His brother points to his weakness when he tells him that a man must be able to judge his own capabilities (23). Madiama's marital situation is similar to that of Mour. Highly dependent on his two wives, he lacks the nobility of mind and strength of purpose of his first wife and the lucidity and ruthlessness of the second. The immediate cause of his deposal is a foolish attempt to assert his independence by snubbing a foreign dignitary, just one more illustration of his lack of judgement. Yelli follows the same pattern of weak protagonists, despite his illustrious ancestors. His irresponsibility with both women and money leaves him bankrupt, with a houseful of children and a resentful first wife desperately trying to support them.

Parallel to these central male figures, there is in each novel a female character who, because of her influence over the course of events, her relationship to the main theme and her power over the apparent protagonist, could be defined as a hidden protagonist. In *Le Revenant* it is Bakar's sister, Yama. She discerns most unequivocally the forces controlling society and sets out to use them to improve her position. Whereas Bakar through his own stupidity becomes a victim, Yama is farsighted and calculating. She embodies most clearly the degradation of social values that Sow Fall is denouncing, but her strength of character and acceptance of responsibility contrast positively with the amiable passivity of her brother. Although the reader reacts negatively to her rejection of Bakar, her behavior is consequential. Yama merely pursues her goals with absolute implacability and her refusal to use *xeesal* symbolizes her lack of hypocrisy and her exceptional nature. Yama's demented reaction to Bakar's reappearance closes the novel on an enigmatic note. Her loss of control, perhaps insanity, may represent a combination of terror and guilt, as well as the shock of her own infallibility. All her well-made plans collapse in that moment. At the same time, the witnesses' acceptance of Bakar's return from the dead is a reminder of the importance in Africa of the continuing relationship between the natural and the supernatural worlds. At the end it could be said that Bakar for the first time consciously assumes an active role in the novel by putting Yama's future in jeopardy. Nevertheless, because of Yama's previous influence on her brother with regard to his crime and then to his revenge, and because of the dynamic way in which she incarnates the values Sow Fall is aiming to expose and condemn, she is at least as important as Bakar in the novel. Yet, although inordinately strong in character and purpose, Yama could not have reached a position of power without her husband's name and money.

In *La Grève des Bàttu* once again a female character stands in opposition to the ambitions of the central figure. Like Yama, Salla Niang is a born leader, and her personality, shrewdness and sense of humor allow her to impose her authority over the beggars. Orphaned at an early age, she has become wise through experience. Mour's hypocrisy towards the beggars annoys her and she deliberately lies to get rid of him. Like Yama, Salla is realistic and has no pity for someone once prepared to sacrifice the beggars for his own needs. The moment Mour leaves, she orders the beggars to stay: "Demain, à cause de nous, il mordra la poussière!" (114) [Tomorrow, we shall see that he bites the dust! (86)]. The novel turns into a trial of strength between Mour and Salla. On his second visit, Mour's desperation (and money) moves some of the beggars, but Salla reminds them they would lose all they have gained in self-respect and social position, if they went into the streets. Because of her opposition Mour cannot carry out the *marabout's* instructions and someone else is appointed vice-president. Thus in Sow Fall's second novel, a woman again plays a primary role. This time she defeats the protagonist, not because she frustrates his ambitions—it is left to the reader to believe or not to believe that—but because she prevents him from manipulating the beggars and forces him to recognize their full status as human beings and as important members of society.

In *L'Appel des arènes*, the conflict is between Nalla and his mother, Diattou. Her struggle to control every aspect of her son's life is an attempt to impose her values. Her final defeat and possible self-destruction or madness underline Diattou's salient role as the embodiment of the most extreme cultural alienation. As such, she could be considered the real protagonist of the novel.

The situation is a little different in *L'Ex-père de la nation* because the disguised protagonist is perhaps more accurately described as the potential protagonist. Madiama's second wife, Yandé, would have been a more successful president than her husband because she understands the realities of power. In alliance with the foreign adviser, Andru, she keeps Madiama in office and protects him from his enemies through her system of spies. She is a diabolic figure, described by him as "une femme qui avait confisqué mon univers à la manière d'une fatalité pesante . . .

insaisissable mais toujours présente dans sa toute puissance incontestable" (40) [a woman who had taken over my world like a burdensome fatality . . . indefinable but always present in her unquestioned omnipotence]. Finally, even Yandé appears impotent in the face of the prolonged drought and ubiquitous corruption driving the impoverished masses to despair. If she had been given a free reign, however, it is conceivable that Yandé would have succeeded through her perspicacity and merciless determination in being kept in power by the foreign governments.

In *Le Jujubier du patriarche*, Naarou symbolizes the survival of tradition in a more active way than Yelli or any other character. She has a mystical relationship with the chant, appearing in her generosity of spirit to be a reincarnation of the slave heroines, Warèle and Biti. Having learnt to recite the whole narrative from the *griot*, Naarou experiences the ancestral exploits as a living message. Furthermore, as she is in reality of both noble and slave descendance, she personifies the necessity for reconciliation. Her refusal to approach Tacko, despite pleas from Yelli and her mother, is not caused by spite, but by the perception that the moment has not yet come. Even before Tacko declares her change of heart at the tomb, Naarou's radiant smile reveals that she knows. Once again, a dynamic female character takes over the most active role in the novel.

These strong women are not without their counterparts among the minor male characters. In *Le Revenant*, Bakar's friend, Sada, represents the survival of integrity and the potential of genuine friendship. The constancy of their relationship is similar to that between Ramatoulaye and Aïssatou in *Une Si Longue Lettre*. Yet in Sow Fall's novel, Sada's strength contrasts with Bakar's weakness: "Sada était un homme méthodique et toujours extrêmement lucide. Il était d'une fermeté inébranlable et ne se laissait jamais entraîner" (38) [Sada was a methodical and extremely lucid man. His determination was unshakable and he never let himself be swayed by others]. Similar to Yama in his individuality and force of character, Sada symbolizes the opposite from her, the survival of virtue in a ruthless society. He stands by Bakar to the end, one of the few genuine mourners at his funeral.

In *La Grève des Bàttu*, Kéba is the strong male figure who stands in contrast to Mour. He takes his work as an agent of the state very seriously and carries it out to the best of his ability and according to his conscience. He is committed to his principles, even if they endanger his advancement and refuses to cooperate with Mour's change of policy on the beggars, shocked by the fact that Mour puts his personal situation above that of the country. As a result, Mour blames his assistant for everything. When Kéba's secretary, Sagar, advises him to conform to the norms of society, even if it means dancing on one foot, he replies: "Si danser d'un pied doit nous précipiter dans un gouffre, je préfère tenir sur mes deux pieds" (100). [If we risk falling down a precipice by dancing on one foot, I prefer to remain on my two feet (75)]. The idea of helping Mour in return for future favors has never occurred to Kéba and he regards such opportunism as a sin against human dignity, like begging. His insistence on giving Sagar's friend a lecture about robbing the state when she asks for gasoline coupons finally convinces Sagar that "Kéba n'est pas comme les autres" (67) [Kéba was different from other people (49)].

Although he is rigid and obsessive, Sow Fall is plainly in agreement with many of Kéba's attitudes. She says in the Hammond interview that Kéba's opinion of begging is perfectly understandable in terms of his upbringing. She even admits that not all beggars are like the ones presented in her novel (195). Whether Kéba is mistaken or not, his integrity is above question, unlike that of Mour. At the same time, his inflexible belief that he is right in condemning begging conflicts with Salla Niang's conviction that the weak have the right to ask for and receive what society has denied them in other ways. Even at the end of the novel, when the beggars are no longer portrayed as parasites but as full citizens, Kéba continues to view them as a scourge. In the indirect confrontation between Salla and Kéba, neither could be said to be right or wrong. Sow Fall presents two valid points of view, dependent on the personal experience of the individual involved.

In *L'Appel des arènes*, because Nalla is weak only by virtue of his childhood and not because of his character, he has no male antithesis, but several men contrast positively with Diattou. Malaw and André represent the traditional Africa she mocks. Yet as country people with little or no formal education, they cannot alone act as role models for urban youth, despite their wisdom and inherited knowledge. The character who matches Diattou in her own domain is Monsieur Niang. Because he is a teacher and an educated man, Diattou assumes that his opinion of African wrestling is the same as hers. He, however, has no problem reconciling the traditional and the modern. He shares Nalla's passion for wrestling, but also sees the necessity for formal studies. He tries to explain that Nalla's fascination is the expression of an unusual aesthetic sensibility, but Ndiogou and Diattou can only relate to the purely rational. Monsieur Niang is not merely a foil to Diattou. His notebook observations on cultural alienation give him special status. His psychological analysis stands outside the main narrative, possessing an objectivity and authority not found elsewhere in the text. Monsieur Niang has a dual function. He is both a participant and an observer, forcing the reader to be the same. The fact that he is always referred to with the title "Monsieur" also endows him with a superiority not conferred on the other characters.

In *L'Ex-père de la nation* two very different male characters stand in opposition to Madiama. His older brother, Bara, represents the moral integrity of traditional values. Gradually the two men become estranged because of Bara's disapproval of Madiama's presidency. In political terms, however, his role is not as instructive as that of the unofficial opposition leader, Dicko. He appears only once in person, near the end of the novel, but is a constant presence from the beginning through his speeches and tracts. From the moment of Independence onwards, Dicko criticizes foreign control of his country and fearlessly speaks out against injustice. He represents a lucid understanding of political reality combined with incorruptible honesty and passionate idealism. Even Madiama's daughter, Nafi, allies herself with Dicko. In the final period of transition to a bloody dictatorship, he is arrested and tortured, becoming internationally famous as a victim of oppression. Nothing intimidates him. Even Andru has to admit defeat: "C'est une espèce d'illuminé" (168) [He's some sort of visionary] and to avoid creating a martyr, Dicko is released.

In *Le Jujubier du patriarche,* Amath, the bookseller in the public gardens, is an exemplary figure for Yelli. Although mistreated by the municipal authorities, Amath's inner serenity contrasts with Yelli's anguish and uncertainty. From the same region and possibly related, the two men develop a special relationship that helps Yelli to reestablish meaningful contact with his roots. The public gardens become his haven of peace. There he can meditate on his life and there he has the flash of inspiration about a pilgrimage. The other symbol of constancy in Yelli's life is the family *griot,* Naani. Once a year he pays a visit, bringing all the news from Babyselli, including that of the buds on the patriarch's tree. Naani dies after the first pilgrimage, his mission completed.

Sow Fall's novels thus reveal that both men and women can have authority, both in the family and the public domain. She shows that individual personality and strength of character, rather than gender, are decisive in the creation and exercise of power. The strong female characters regard themselves as the equals of men and take their own emancipation for granted, never discussing the rights of women. Sow Fall could have chosen to portray the same characteristics through men. She does not use her main female characters to protest against the injustices of the feminine condition. Rather, they reveal the power and therefore potential equality of women in Senegalese society. In this sense, Sow Fall could be described as a feminist of a different type from Bâ. She demonstrates that the position of women is not necessarily inferior to that of men and is sometimes superior. Some women have the same capacity to control or shape their community as men and must therefore accept the same responsibility for their actions. Yama, Salla, Diattou, Yandé, and Naarou do not only represent their own gender. They embody aspects of contemporary Senegalese society important to all its members.

Yet Sow Fall is also aware that the traditionally compliant role assigned to women in Africa is problematic. When questioned by Hammond, Sow Fall rejects the anti-male attitude of some western feminists and stresses the need for women to be taught the role of full citizens (194). The importance of education is revealed in *Le Revenant* through Mame Aïssa, but in her case a traditional education has served to create and reinforce her docility: "L'éducation a l'étrange pouvoir de modeler l'individu selon des normes inviolables et de le rendre quasi impuissant dans toute tentative de se libérer de ces normes." (63) [Education has the strange power to model an individual according to inviolable norms and to make that individual almost powerless in any attempt at liberation from those norms]. A European-style education may be an instrument of emancipation. The university student, Raabi, in *La Grève des Bàttu* is a parallel figure to Daba in *Une Si Longue Lettre*, passionately intellectual, naturally independent and assertive. Even before her father takes a second wife, she is an ardent opponent of polygamy. Her disappointment at her mother's passivity and her growing disgust for her father are in flagrant revolt against the traditional role of a daughter.

Although Sow Fall is obviously sympathetic towards Raabi's point of view, she does not condemn Lolli. Like Bâ, she portrays the difference in mentality between the generations, but also shows that each woman must base her decisions on her own evaluation of the situation and conception of duty. This tolerance also explains her compassionate treatment of Mame Aïssa. In her article "Du Pilon à la Machine à écrire" [From the Pestle to the Typewriter], Sow Fall praises the tendency of African women to forge their own destiny. She refers to Ramatoulaye's acceptance of polygamy for her children's sake as a noble decision, as noble as that to be free (77). In the final sentence of the article, she sums up her attitude to the emancipation of women, claiming that she is only in favor of freedom if it is obtained with dignity and propriety (77).

The Use of Irony

Sow Fall's characters are not presented as models to be imitated, although some are positive and others negative. Rather they illustrate the multiplicity of types to be found in Senegal. This is a society assailed by contradictions because of the transition from traditional to modern life as well as from colonization to Independence, an independence that can hardly be complete in this age of a world economy and universal western culture. Sow Fall avoids ideological discourse, using irony to expose the ambiguity and contradictions she sees. Underlying all her novels are a number of basic ironies, which serve to reveal and emphasize her social criticism.

Bakar does not believe in social and material ambitions, but through his love for his wife and family, he subscribes to them and eventually commits a crime to fulfill them. In addition, he steals for a woman who genuinely loves him and who does not appear to care for money. Bakar condemns hypocrisy and self-interest as symbolized by *xeesal* and the funeral broadcasts, but uses both as instruments of his revenge. A social outcast after his imprisonment, he is made into a celebrity by his funeral bulletin and ceremony. He criticizes the practice of turning funerals into a financial transaction, but this very practice makes a rich man of him at the end. Money is thus both the downfall and salvation of Bakar. In both instances the money is stolen, although in the second case it is perhaps rightfully his.

In *La Grève des Bàttu*, the irony is even more biting. It is created through a multiplicity of viewpoints casting each situation in a different light according to the individual judging it. Mour directs the campaign to remove the beggars, the success of which he considers to be the cause of his ultimate failure. Kéba carries out the operation but then refuses to reverse it. That is, the person who has contributed most to Mour's political achievements in the past, becomes, in the opinion of both Mour and Lolli, the most significant obstacle to his supreme promotion. In the beginning, both Mour and Kéba want to get rid of the beggars, not only because they have been instructed to do so by their superiors, but also for personal reasons. Mour perceives an opportunity for advancement, while Kéba is delighted to combine duty and pleasure to eliminate a social blight. For the same personal reasons, Mour wants the return of the beggars, but Kéba declines to enact it. The very integrity and dedication that have hitherto made Kéba an excellent assistant irrevocably exclude his continued cooperation with Mour. Kéba cannot agree to a personal enterprise conflicting in his opinion with the good of the State as well as his own convictions.

The relationship between Mour and the beggars is also treated in an ironic way. He lies to the beggars, but cannot believe they would lie to him. He is indifferent to their predicament, but is shocked by the fact they are indifferent to his. At first he is the power controlling their fate. Then they become the power controlling his. In the end, he becomes a beggar himself. The final irony with regard to Mour's relationships with others is exposed in the last sentence of the novel. The minister he despises and expects to defeat is made vice-president instead of him.

The association between the beggars and the rest of society goes through a similar reversal. At first, the beggars struggle desperately against their exclusion from public life. Then they exclude themselves and a movement develops to bring them back. From a humiliated and oppressed group, treated as sub-humans by the authorities and forced to accept whatever is handed to them, they develop into proud and free citizens, establishing their own rules with regard to charity. Society can function without the likes of Mour, but the disappearance of the beggars results in chaos. Sometimes classed as parasites, they are revealed to contribute as much as they take.

The use of irony is not confined to situations and relationships. It also illuminates contradictions and ambiguities within the individual. Mour claims to reject the beggars, despite their traditional place in society, in the name of science and progress. Yet he regards polygamy as his historic right and has an unshakable belief in the infallibility of *marabouts*. Although the use of irony is centered on Mour, it is not exclusive to him. The self-righteous Kéba is conducting a liaison with his secretary, although he is married. Salla Niang, theoretically doubly oppressed by her position as a beggar and a woman, has unlimited freedom compared to Lolli, the wife of the politician.

The use of irony in *La Grève des Bàttu* is sometimes entertaining, because the basic situation has its amusing as well as its disturbing aspects. This humor is absent from the irony in *L'Appel des arènes* where Diattou's situation is finally tragic.   Normally, the older generation is attached to tradition and is forced to defend it against the assaults of the young. In this novel, the youngest character embraces tradition in opposition to his parents. Conventionally, parents are wise and teach their children. Nalla's parents are blind, but the boy instinctively goes in the right direction. They reject wrestling as barbaric, until Ndiogou witnesses the passionate interest of the highly educated, eminent personalities of both races among the spectators. He ultimately realizes that it is possible to be committed to a form of progress without abandoning his own culture. For Diattou there is no such solution. She spurns community life because it curtails her freedom as a "modern" woman. Yet, the community eventually rejects her, so that she is not even free to carry out the work she loves. Diattou is dedicated to her family, but her intransigence takes them away from her, too. At the end she is engulfed by a solitude of her own creation. It threatens to destroy her sanity and perhaps her life, but, unlike her husband, she finds it impossible to change.

The most immediate irony in *L'Ex-père de la nation* lies in the title. Normally speaking, it is impossible to be an ex-father. The original honorary title was ironic too, because, despite Madiama's desire to be a genuine father to his country, the epithet never represented the reality of presidential power. Another basic irony exists in the central symbol of the novel. Madiama compared himself to the sun, but at the beginning of his memoirs he understands the foolishness of the comparison. The sun will rise again, but not Madiama, now examining the dark labyrinth of his conscience (8). A series of ironies are integral to his life story. He achieves more in his fight for justice as a nobody than he does as president. The force of collective action contrasts with the powerlessness of an individual isolated from his people. A victim of oppression in his young days as a labor agitator, he becomes an oppressor himself after his daughter's death, even banning the unions he helped to establish. Madiama long retains the illusion that he has some freedom, but he is not even at liberty to resign when he understands the true nature of his regime. Imprisoned as a young militant by the colonial authorities, he returns to prison as a president discarded by the former colonial power. The use of first person narrative is essentially ironic. Madiama gives the reader information with implications beyond his understanding at the time. For example, he thinks he controls Andru, but the reader understands from the first few pages the insidious influence of the foreign advisor. Of course, as he is writing his memoirs, Madiama also benefits from hindsight, so there is a double irony in the distance between the disillusioned Madiama and the inexperienced idealist and that between the reader and the two stages of Madiama. He recreates his former naivety so vividly, however, that the reader sometimes forgets that the narrator is the deposed and imprisoned president and relishes the illusion of superior knowledge.

The use of irony is gentler and less obvious in *Le Jujubier du patriarche*. In a world obsessed with progress, it is paradoxical that the solution to the clan problems lies in the reestablishment of a living link with events that took place seven hundred years ago. Furthermore, the true heroines of the epic chant turn out to be the two slavewomen, who sacrificed their lives to make the noble quest succeed. The only modern heroines in the novel, Naarou and her mother, Penda, are also considered of slave descent, although in fact they are partly of noble blood. Tacko and Yelli cling to the caste system as the only shred of honor left in their fallen situation, because they have misunderstood the meaning of the relationships within the clan. The clan is not based on a power struggle, but on mutual support and reciprocal affection and on a common concept of honor and dignity.

With regard to form, there is an evolution in Sow Fall's writing towards a more relaxed style and a distinctively African mixture. She uses a sprinkling of Wolof and Wolofized Arabic in all the novels, especially marked in the speech of the beggars in *La Grève des Bàttu*. It is used to denote dress, food, customs and virtues, as well as to express greetings, exclamations and Wolof proverbs. The desire to create a more specifically African form is clearest in *Le Jujubier du patriarche*, where dialogue is more prominent and where the epic poem covers a total of twenty pages, mostly at the end. Yet Sow Fall has great flexibility of style. She moves between informal conversation and formal third-person narrative according to her purpose. In *L'Appel des arènes* and *L'Ex-père de la nation*, the importance of formal narrative reflects the distance between the narrator and the events recounted, the resulting objectivity illuminating the central dilemma. In *La Grève des Bàttu* and *Le Jujubier du patriarche,* the dialogue with Wolof words and speech patterns brings the characters to life in all their cultural specificity, while making the novels more accessible to an African readership.

As each of Sow Fall's novels examines a different social and psychological dilemma, it is difficult to establish an indisputable evolution in content. Her overriding concern appears to be the identity crisis and lack of freedom resulting from cultural conflict and political and economic pressures. She reveals her conviction that the problems depicted are not confined to Senegal by refusing to be geographically precise except in *Le Revenant* and *L'Appel des arènes*. The identity crisis affects all Africans, whether they are conscious of it or not. The Nigerian critic, Femi Ojo-Ade claims that one of the main problems in present-day Africa is "how to remain black in a world becoming whiter every day" (86). Although she may agree with Ojo-Ade's assertion, Sow Fall formulates it differently. The total rejection of traditional ways is a destructive course, both for the individual and society. At the same time, it is impossible to ignore the irreversible changes that have taken place in Africa in recent years. There is no going back to a past that no longer exists. In their joint article, she and Rose Senghor expound the necessity for a combination of the best of the old and the new (239). Although she appears to weigh both equally, Sow Fall's sympathies lie on the side of tradition. It can hardly be a matter of chance that of her five female protagonists, the two who triumph (Salla Niang and Naarou) are undeniable representatives of tradition.

There are no simple answers, only possibilities, and Sow Fall's work offers enlightening situations rather than specific solutions. In the Hammond interview, she defines her role as suggestive rather than prescriptive. Her novels, she says, are an invitation to reflection (192). Yet certain convictions reveal themselves clearly in the texts. The cure for social ills must be based on a belief in the community and be rooted in the mutual respect of all human beings for each other. There is a famous Wolof proverb often found in Senegalese writing and which appears twice in *L'Appel des arènes*, although expressed slightly differently each time: "L'homme n'a qu'un remède, et c'est l'homme" (115) and "L'homme est le remède de l'homme" (131) [Mankind's only remedy is mankind]. To ignore this tenet is to court a living death. This is the essential message of Sow Fall's writing.

V

Other Women Writers

At this stage, Diallo, Bâ, and Sow Fall are considered the major women novelists from Senegal, but they are not alone. A number of other women have published one work, or in the case of Aminata Maïga Ka, two *nouvelles dramatiques* [story dramas] published in one volume and one novel. These books need to be situated in terms of the development of the Senegalese novel by women. In the "Vies d'Afrique" series, of which *De Tilène au Plateau* was the first, there is *Le Baobab fou* by Ken Bugul (1982) and *Collier de cheville* by Adja Ndèye Boury Ndiaye (1983). These were followed by Mame Seck Mbacke's *Le Froid et le piment: Nous travailleurs immigrés* (1983), Catherine N'Diaye's *Gens de sable* (1984) and Aminata Maïga Ka's *La Voie du salut/Le Miroir de la vie* (1985). In 1989 two more novels appeared: Maïga Ka's *En Votre Nom et au mien* and Khadi Fall's *Mademba*. Finally, *La Mauvaise Passe* by Aïcha Diouri was published in 1990.

These books are written by women from different generations and cover a timespan of two decades in terms of their conception, but there is a remarkable communality of themes as well as a close relationship in content to the novels already discussed. Like Diallo, Bâ and Sow Fall, all these women bear witness to a society in turbulent transition. Only Bugul's book is an overt autobiography, but there are autobiographical elements in the works by Adja Ndèye Ndiaye and Catherine N'Diaye. In addition, Mbacke's writing is essentially an account of her own experiences with Senegalese immigrants in France.

Le Baobab fou is a passionate, poetic and, in the context of African feminine literature, a surprising account of a young woman's experiences in Belgium, with significant flashbacks to her previous life in Senegal. Although the book opens with a double prologue entitled "Préhistoire de Ken" and "Histoire de Ken," describing in third-person narrative the establishment of her family and her own birth in a village in the interior of Senegal, the main story, written in the first person, begins with Bugul's departure for "le Nord Terre Promise" (33) [the Promised Land North (23)[14]] and ends with her return to the village. Within that main section there are two flashbacks, one short (79–82) and one long (129–171), revealing the childhood and youth of the narrator before her departure for Europe.

Without the autobiographical label, *Le Baobab fou* would be taken for fiction, partly because of the dramatic nature of the events described, but also, as with Diallo's *De Tilène au Plateau*, because of the lack of emphasis on concrete facts. The exceptions are the names of the streets where the narrator lives in Brussels, the name of her birthplace and occasionally her age. Only one date is revealed and that indirectly. Bugul says the Festival of Negro Arts took place when she was sixteen or seventeen. This event of 1966 allows the reader to work out a vague chronology. Otherwise *Le Baobab fou* is a highly subjective presentation of one woman's search for the meaning of life. Only in Belgium are people given names. In the Senegalese episodes, the characters remain shadowy, even symbolic, figures, so that the main focus is always on the feelings and thoughts of the narrator.

The poetic use of language also relates closely to a style of writing associated with fiction. The frequent interjections or prayer-like incantations, lamenting the absence of the village and the loss of the mother, create an interweaving of the past and present throughout the text. Bernard Magnier highlights the question of form and genre in his 1985 interview with Bugul. He asks her if the work is a novel and she tells him that the label is of no importance. Whatever the genre, everything comes from inside the writer: "L'essentiel est que l'on s'exprime. C'est tout." (154) [The essential element is self-expression. That's all]. These remarks support George May's basic assertion that the only difference between a novel and an autobiography lies in the attitude of the reader. He claims, like Bugul, that for the writer, the two activities appear to be the same (178).

Bugul's lack of interest in genre terminology is probably occasioned by her reasons for writing as well as the perspective of the older Bugul in relation to her younger self. She explains in the Magnier interview that she had no intention of producing a book but started to record her experiences as a form of therapy (151). She showed the manuscript to her compatriot, the writer Annette Mbaye d'Erneville, who immediately took it to a publisher. Bugul points out that, although *Le Baobab fou* appeared in 1982, it actually described her life of ten years previously and was written between 1972 and 1979–80. In the meantime she had accumulated other, completely different lives, as she herself expresses it (152). Although *Le Baobab fou* belongs to the "Vies d'Afrique" series published by les Nouvelles Editions Africaines and is, according to the editors, a true biographical account, N.E.A. refused to allow the author to use her own name, Mariétou M'Baye. They were afraid that some African readers would be scandalized by the life depicted. She was, however, permitted to choose her own pseudonym and explains to Magnier that "Ken Bugul" is the name given by mothers to a child born after a number of still-births. It means "Nobody wants it" and is supposed to protect the child from death (153). This choice reflects the narrator's view of her early abandonment, but it may also be an ironic indication of the distance between the writer at the moment of publication and the younger narrator. This distance can be seen in the first sentence of the main section, otherwise in the first person: "Ken Bugul se souvient" (33). [Ken Bugul remembers (23)]. In a literal sense the author and the main character are identical. Yet psychologically and emotionally Bugul has entered a new stage of her existence by the time the book is finished. In addition to the distinction between the older and younger

Bugul, there is another dichotomy within the text. The child/young woman has two distinct voices, representing the conflicts tearing her apart at the time: the factual outer voice recounting the events in the life of an apparently docile child and confident young woman and the poetic inner voice expressing her fears, longings and the anguish of her memories. In the Magnier interview Bugul reveals that after Belgium she spent seven years in France. Yet at the end of *Le Baobab fou* Ken goes straight back to Senegal and to the village. The reader has the impression that her European experience is over and that she has returned definitively to her roots. This conclusion gives the book an artistic unity that did not exist in Bugul's life. As she points out to Magnier: "Moi, je n'ai pas fini de vivre. J'ai plus d'années devant moi que derrière moi" (154). [I, myself, haven't stopped living. I have more years in front of me than behind me].

Although there is an illusion of unity associated with fiction, *Le Baobab fou* is undoubtedly an autobiography. As Dorothy Blair points out (1984:121), Bugul could easily have used the same material to produce a novel, but she chose to retain the form of her original writings. The fact that *Le Baobab fou* describes real-life experiences is of the greatest importance, both to herself and her readership, particularly in Africa. Before publication, Bugul believed her ordeal unique, but was determined to produce an honest account under her own name. When Magnier asks Bugul if she has revealed what others felt obliged to suppress, she says that only after publication did she discover that other women had similar problems and adds: "Je sais que je leur ai rendu service. En me libérant, je les ai libérés" (152). [I know that I did them a service. While freeing myself, I freed them]. She talks to Magnier of the shocked reaction of many Senegalese to such a book written by a village woman, a Moslem and daughter of a marabout. Some refused to believe it was a true story. Yet, because of its candor, as well as the talent of the author, *Le Baobab fou* has an original place in African literature. As the author herself says: "Ce livre aide certains à sortir d'une routine, d'une certaine forme de littérature africaine, de certaines idées ou d'une façon d'écrire" (154). [This books helps some people to abandon certain rigid ideas about the form and content of African literature]. Still, an anonymous review in *Jeune Afrique*, presumably aimed at Africans, seems to imply that *Le Baobab fou* needs an apologia and ends on the following rather unusual note: "Décidément, Ken Bugul est bien sympathique" (72). [Undoubtably, Ken Bugul is very likeable].

Adja Ndèye Boury Ndiaye's *Collier de cheville* reminds us of Diallo's *De Tilène au Plateau*. Focussing on a character called Tante Lika, it is an account of life in the Plateau area of Dakar before Independence, although most of the action takes place before and during the Second World War. Guyonneau in her bibliography calls it the autobiography of a midwife, but this point of view is not clear from the text, written in the third person except for one "je" (71), revealing nothing of the identity of the narrator. The blurb on the back of the book cover describes the text as a young girl's memories enhanced by a Lebou woman's sensitivity, but there is no-one in the work with the same name as the author, nor is there a midwife in the family treated in the book. Yet, as *Collier de cheville* is included in the "Vies d'Afrique" series, the reader must assume that it is the biography of a real person.

As a piece of creative writing it is not a success, tending to fall into long-winded documentary. The blurb praises the detailed culinary and vestimentary references, but the result of the overabundance of cultural detail is that *Collier de cheville* hovers somewhere between creative writing and the recording of facts. The *African Book Publishing Record* has the same problem with classification. In its book review section it includes *Collier de cheville* under "Sociology", not "Literature." Esther Smith does not concur with my harsh judgement, however. She sees a virtue where I indicate a short-coming: "The special contribution of this work is the concrete detail, the almost cinematographic description of everyday events, sights, colors and sounds" (29).

Apart from the inclination towards meticulous documentary, the characters are wooden and the work lacks conviction as a depiction of human relationships. Roger Dorsinville reveals in a review of the "Vies d'Afrique" series that in general *Collier de cheville* has been severely criticized for its lack of literary worth. He claims that this is fallacious criticism based on irrelevant European standards and that the book is irreplaceable as a portrayal of a period of transition in African life (150). Literary value is a subject one could argue about for ever and, despite my negative opinion of Ndiaye's book from a literary standpoint, it is worth examining in the context of this study because of its content. It cannot be discussed as an autobiography, however, because there are no autobiographical indications in the text.

Mame Seck Mbacke spent many years living in France, both as a student and as a social worker. After completing a doctorate in Economic and Social Development, she worked for seven years at the Senegalese Consulate-General in Paris, dealing with the social problems of Senegalese immigrants. *Le Froid et le piment*, reflects this experience, being a mixture of documentation and fiction. Guyonneau mistakenly calls it autobiography. It is actually the presentation of other people's lives. The first half consists of thirty-three case studies from several lines to several pages in length, some in the first, some in the third person. In the second half there are two pieces of fiction. The first is a short story twenty pages long called "Un homme de couleur raconte" dealing with the life and eventual murder of a young African man, resident in Paris. It begins in the first person, presenting the point of view of the protagonist's younger brother, slips into the third person on the second page where the brother seemingly disappears and returns to the first-person on the last page. This narrative construction is artificial and unsatisfying and the story itself is underdeveloped as a character study. Yet it succeeds in painting a stark, somber picture of French life for single immigrant men from North and Black Africa, plainly reflecting the prime intent of the author. The second story, "Youmané, l'Africaine exilée" is three times the length and more interesting as a piece of creative writing. It opens with a short presentation of Youmané in France, then returns to her childhood in a Senegalese village, describing how her desire for excitement leads her to Dakar and finally Paris. At the end, she dies abandoned and ruined by her white husband's rejection. I found it a moving story, but Thomas O'Toole considers it full of clichés and after the move to Paris "stock melodrama" which "lacks both artistic and social science value" (227). The two halves of *Le Froid et le piment* spring from the same source and Youmané's story appears to be a reconstructed fictional version of the case-study entitled "Confession" in the first part of the book (73). The keynote throughout is tragedy. Mbacke chose to highlight the plight of African immigrants in France, marooned in a hostile world.

Catherine N'Diaye's *Gens de sable* is quite different in form from any of the other works in this study. It is a series of poetic tableaux or, in her words, "rêveries pensantes" (95) [thoughtful reveries], combining observation and imagination to produce an individual but authentic vision of Senegalese reality. The situation of the author is also quite different. Having grown up in France with a Senegalese father and a German mother and a minimal knowledge of Wolof, N'Diaye is nonetheless fascinated by her African heritage and by Senegal. A journalist, also interested in the problems of the immigrant community, her writings reflect her French education, whether in the scholarly references to Tournier (68) or the theories of Baudrillard (71) or in the peculiarly French analytic thinking or in the very language she uses. Yet I consider her book to belong to the literature of Senegal, both because of its subject matter and because of the self-identification of the author with Senegal. She is at pains to establish the strength of her links with Africa, first with a pointed reference to her name at the very beginning of the book, then with a description of her relationship with her grandmother and an emphasis on blood ties (9). The title of the work, too, refers to her own family, from the north of Senegal bordering on the desert.

N'Diaye's perception of Africa is a privileged one precisely because she is both insider and outsider. In a footnote she explains her decision not to correct an unintentional use of both "here" and "there" to refer to Senegal, deciding it reflects her true situation: "l'ambiguïté de l'appartenance à distance" (17). [the ambiguity of belonging at a distance]. She feels she has the subjectivity of the emotional participant and the objectivity of the cool observer (15). Paradoxically, her insight is heightened at times by her non-comprehension of the language. Her reveries focus on the aesthetic aspects of daily life in Senegal. Even the most prosaic activities have a magic and a mystery because "la spiritualité est mêlée à toute la vie" (48) [spirituality is a part of everything] and because of the innate artistry of the people, creating works of art out of the ordinary elements of their lives, such as cars or market displays or hairstyles. Much of what she describes has a surreal quality, such as the gardens festooned with the plastic remains from the Bata factory, or Jean-Paul's house in the south painted with a mother-of-pearl liquid from boiled shells. Fairy-tale and mythical elements are prominent. The beautiful Yama Sow is an ogress who devours men (23). On the grave of the cruel tyrant, Salmone Faye, a red pepper, symbol of suffering, grows and survives all droughts (97). The aesthetic approach of N'Diaye does not, however, attempt to mask a sadder reality. Her book is an illuminating view of Africa and of the dilemma of all poor countries.

Aminata Maïga Ka is the wife of the established playwright and short story writer, Abdou Anta Ka. *La Voie du salut / Le Miroir de la vie* appeared in 1985 but, according to the dates at the end of the text, she wrote the first story between 1977 and 1980, making her a contemporary of Diallo, Bâ, and Sow Fall. Her work, more than that of the other women in this section, reminds us of the novels of Bâ and Sow Fall, because of the focus on the position of women and on current social problems. Ka proclaims her admiration for Bâ in the dedication to the second story: "A ma fille Mariama Ba Ka, afin qu'elle puisse hériter les qualités de coeur et d'esprit de sa grande homonyme." [To my daughter, Mariama Ba Ka, so that she may inherit the qualities of heart and mind of her great namesake]. *En Votre Nom et au mien* was written in 1986/87 and continues the underlying debate of the first stories about the relationship between tradition and modernity, particularly with regard to marriage.

All three works use third-person narrative with multiple viewpoints, but in each text the thoughts and attitudes of the female protagonists are privileged. *La Voie du salut* opens with the voice of an older woman who has just died. Her thoughts return to her youth and we discover she is Rokhaya, a Toucouleur from the interior. The text recounts her marriage, the birth of her daughter, Rabiatou, and the daughter's marriage. It is not until almost the end of the narrative that Rokhaya's death takes place, to be followed by that of Rabiatou. This circular construction serves to remind the reader from the beginning, like the title [the road to salvation], that no one is immortal and that this life is merely the means to salvation in the next.

In terms of main themes, both stories could be called "La Vie" [life], although the first points to life after death and the second title, *Le Miroir de la vie*, stresses the realistic presentation of this life. Both share a tragic vision of the position of women in modern Senegal. The second story was written in 1983 and covers a time span of about a year in the same period. It is a chronological account of a *nouveau riche* family focussing on Fatou, the maid. The work opens and closes with her situation, excluding an epilogue in the form of a letter. Each character represents a different age, social, or ideological group and Ka skillfully explores the complexity of modern Africa from varying viewpoints.

The title of *En Votre Nom et au mien* reveals the greater militancy of Ka in her latest work. The novel recounts chronologically the two marriages of Awa, the protagonist. The first, to an older, rich man she does not love, is polygamous. The second is a monogamous love match with her original partner of choice. Although Ka undeniably opts for freedom of choice, once again the use of multiple viewpoints emphasizes the complexity of decision-making in a value system in transition.

Mademba is ostensibly the autobiography of a nineteen-year-old man of the same name, transcribed from cassettes he recorded in hospital, while believing himself to be terminally ill with throat cancer. The narrator says his illness gives him the distance to write about himself as though he were another person (92). In addition, convinced his childhood and youth are representative, he is anxious to record them before his voice or his life runs out. This pseudo-autobiographical framework to the novel is provided in a short explanatory introduction and is presumably designed to lend greater authenticity to the text. The narrative proper consists of twenty-three chapters, largely in the first person with the occasional use by Mademba of the third person to talk about himself. Each chapter appears to represent a daily recording session. In chapter 12, however, the authorial voice intervenes to give the reader information unknown to the narrator. Mademba's tumor has mysteriously disappeared, but he refuses to believe he is cured, convinced there is a plot to hide the truth. During the second half of the novel, the delusion that he is condemned to death creates an ironic distance between the reader and the narrator, making the reader privileged and increasing the fascination of the text. In the final chapter Mademba accepts the fact he is cured and leaves the hospital with a new-found independence and strength.

A few snatches of news from a hospital radio situate the events in 1988, but the narrative moves around freely in time, slowly constructing a full account of Mademba's previous life while remaining firmly rooted in the present. Sent from the country to a Coranic school in the capital at the age of five, Mademba escapes and makes a life for himself, first as a street child and then in the rich family of his mother's cousin. This broad sweep enables Fall to focus on many aspects of Senegalese society, often with a critical eye. Although the narrator is a man, the most interesting character of the novel is his female cousin, Faatim. She is seventeen years older than Mademba but is his closest friend, visiting him every day in the hospital. Parallel to the discovery of his past life, there is the gradual unfolding of her unorthodox and intriguing story, not complete until the final pages of the text. Through Faatim, Khadi Fall exposes the social problems of a woman who refuses to conform.

La Mauvaise Passe is unusual in that its author, Aïcha Diouri was only fifteen when she wrote it and sixteen at the time of publication.

Although called a novel on the title page, it is only sixty-five pages in length, but as Lilyan Kesteloot points out in her introduction, it is a courageous attempt to expose a serious social problem in the form of a fictional account. Like Khadi Fall, Diouri champions the rights of children, in particular those away from the protection of their family. In a third person narrative privileging the point of view of the boy protagonist, she describes the rejection and fall of Alioune in the first half of the text and his salvation and rehabilitation in a children's home in the second.

Women and Society

Despite obvious differences, the similarities between these eight works are striking. All are consciously or unconsciously committed to a sociological or ethnographic point of view and all except *La Mauvaise Passe* give special attention to the lives of women. Yet they do not all present the same image of women. Catherine N'Diaye and Adja Ndèye Ndiaye wish to defend the point of view that women are traditionally powerful and influential members of society. Catherine N'Diaye talks of "un matriarcat tenace qui survit sous des rituels islamiques de surface" (26) [a tenacious matriarchy which survives under superficial Islamic rituals] and refers to Senegal as a patriarchy only in appearance. She supports the view that the sexual differentiation in traditional life has been misrepresented as a power differentiation by those who would like to prove that colonization did not change the power structure. The head of the N'Diaye family is her grandmother, Mam' Naffy, whose relationship with Catherine is like that between Safi and Mame in *De Tilène au Plateau*. Mam' Naffy is the powerful matriarch, head of a united family living inside and outside Senegal. She is a colorful, obstinate but wise old woman, "extrêmement ferme dans ses propos" (8) [extremely firm in her opinions]. Many characters are presented briefly in *Gens de sable* but she is the one remaining most clearly in the mind of the reader.

Tante Lika in *Collier de cheville* resembles Mam' Naffy in her force of character and in the matriarchal role she plays in the family. Treated with great deference by her husband, she is considered to have special powers, symbolized by her anklet. Yet the other women are relegated to a passive and inferior role compared to the men. The result is a conflict in the novel between the depiction of Lika, an affirmation of female authority, and that of the remaining female characters, lacking her power of choice.

The other writers present a different and generally more complex picture of the family and of the place of women, but the woman as mother is a central figure in all the texts. In *La Mauvaise Passe*, Alioune's mother is almost too horrible to be true and her portrait belies the traditional African image of maternal devotion. She neglects, starves, and insults her youngest son and allows him to be beaten and humiliated by the rest of the family. In the works of Bugul, Mbacke, Ka, and Fall, the mother is presented positively, but does not have the matriarchal authority of Mam' Naffy and Tante Lika. She is the long-suffering, hard-working, self-effacing but loving victim, common in African literature. The mothers of Youmané and of the maid, Fatou, in *Le Miroir de la vie*, Rokhaya in *La Voie du salut*, Awa's mother in *En Votre Nom et au mien* and Mademba's mother all follow this pattern. Although submissive to their husbands, these women play an irreplaceable role in their children's lives, giving and inspiring undying affection. Mademba's mother died when he was five, but she continues to be a living and loving presence in his mind. His story opens with a dream about her from the previous day.

Ken Bugul's mother is also of primary importance in her daughter's life, not because of unqualified reciprocal love, but because Ken sees her as the fundamental cause of her feeling of solitude. Ken's alienation is represented by the recurring symbol of the amber bead the two-year-old child pushed into her ear, but the bead is only a precursor of the mother's departure several years later. Although they are reunited after one year, the mother had already transferred her affections to a new grandchild and Ken says "*ma* mère n'était plus" (130) [*my* mother was no longer (112)]. The damage to the child is permanent: "Je maudirai toute ma vie ce jour qui avait emporté ma mère, qui m'avait écrasé l'enfance" (81) [All my life I shall curse the day that carried my mother off, that shattered my childhood (66)]. Lamentations about the loss of the mother and incantations addressing the mother are a leitmotif of *Le Baobab fou*, erupting in the text whenever the narrator feels powerless or anguished.

Although the mother as embodiment of love or lack of love is prominent in all the books, the function of the mother as a contrast to her daughter is perhaps more significant, considering the protagonistic role of young women. The lives of the older generation offer little choice, especially with respect to marriage, the principle element in a traditional woman's life. Their daughters are confronted with a changing society giving greater freedom, but this freedom entails decisions, conflicts, and sometimes cultural alienation. In *La Voie du salut*, the dual account of Rokhaya and Rabiatou forces the reader to compare the two. When Rokhaya marries, she accepts her uncle's assertion that henceforth she belongs body and soul to her husband (36), but she feels lonely and neglected in marriage. Later, when her daughter asserts her individualism, Rokhaya feels overtaken by events. Although understanding Rabiatou's desire to marry for love, she is shocked by the young woman's refusal to consider a dowry and appalled when Rabiatou deliberately becomes pregnant to avoid it. Rabiatou regards such traditional attitudes and customs as unnecessary complications and as symptoms of social retardation. Like the young couples in the novels of Bâ and Sow Fall, she and her husband, Racine, want their union to be based on equality and honesty. Yet Rabiatou soon finds herself neglected, just like her mother. She thinks of leaving Racine, but stays because of the children, the prospect of polygamy never crossing her mind. In a tragic denouement reminiscent of *Un Chant écarlate*, she collapses and dies when hearing of her husband's second marriage. Rabiatou thought she could control her own life. The irony is that she is as much at the mercy of her husband as her mother was.

The ambiguity disappears in Ka's latest work, where she firmly opts for love and freedom of choice. In agreeing to her first marriage, Awa is faithful to her traditional upbringing of obedience without question, but she finally revolts against living for others and the marriage ends in divorce. Fortunately, her first love, Demba, now has an important position and the second marriage is welcomed by Awa's family. Her future life will not be easy, however, and the last words of the novel, "je continuerai la lutte" [I will continue the fight] affirm the need for women to demand the happiness and justice to which they have a right. Ka shows that it is impossible to impose traditional marital values on a world into which education and global communications have introduced a different mentality.

Ken Bugul resembles Rabiatou in her level of education and feminist consciousness, although she is a more fully developed and complex personality. She too rejects her mother's traditional place in society, described as that of witness to the superior role of the man (146). Influenced by western schooling and her own isolation, she embarks on the individualistic course that leads her abroad. In Belgium she meets the Italian, Léonora, who awakens her feminist aspirations. In the desperation of her search for self-identity and communication with others, she exploits the sexual power she exerts as a beautiful black woman in a white society that sometimes treats her as a luxury consumer product. The end result is a traumatic experience and her return to Senegal. Although her life as an African woman in Europe is primordial in the book, one aspect of Ken's revolt is the desire to throw off all the constraints normally imposed on women in her own country. Her story exposes the dilemma of the modern woman caught between two worlds, neither offering permanent refuge.

Mbacke's Youmané is also unwilling to follow in the footsteps of her mother. From an early age she rebels against household tasks and with "une nature particulièrement masculine" (115) prefers to accompany her father to the fields. Yet finally only the city interests her. Mbacke says: "elle était née pour combattre et vaincre" (131) [she was born to fight and conquer] and talks of her inordinate ambition (131) but Youmané strikes the reader as a foolish young girl dazzled by dreams of a glamorous world. Despite making a new life for herself in Dakar, she is never again genuinely happy and becomes a permanent exile, first in her own country and then in France. Unlike Rabiatou and Ken, however, she has no feminist consciousness and does not analyze her life. Notwithstanding her desire to escape from the life her mother led, Youmané finally reveals the same resignation as the older woman. Ironically, her freedom destroys her. At least her mother is secure in her traditional environment and she survives.

Faatim in *Mademba* is different from the other female characters. Sent to study in France where she received a doctorate in sociology, she fell in love with a Senegalese of the *griot* caste, who abandoned her after the birth of their child. Totally unconventional and in revolt against social niceties and expected behavior, she lives in the family villa, but is treated as a marginal creature, everyone calling her "Faatim, la folle" [the madwoman]. Her mother, the acquiescent first wife of Mademba's uncle, feels hostile towards this daughter with whom she has nothing in common and Faatim abhors and despises the prevailing petty-mindedness and hypocrisy her mother shares. Yet Faatim is a positive character. She is naturally kind, helping the street boy Mademba, and later bringing him into the household, after discovering his identity through a family photograph. At one stage Faatim considers marrying again, but finally rejects matrimony as incompatible with her need for freedom. Although brilliant, her unorthodox ideas make it difficult for her to acquire and retain work and it would be problematic for her to survive without her father's money. In Faatim's case, it seems inappropriate to talk about a generation conflict with her mother. Mentally they inhabit separate worlds and do not communicate. Another woman in *Mademba* is a free spirit, but within the system. Aja Nabu, the third wife of Mademba's uncle, succeeds in reestablishing herself after choosing divorce from her first husband because he took a young girl as a second wife. Beautiful and astute, she refuses to remain a victim. She knows how to manipulate men and marries again on her own terms.

The younger women depicted in this last group of novels are not a homogeneous group and their destinies are not the same. Yet in general, they reveal the dangers inherent in freedom of choice, particularly with regard to love and marriage. Despite the sympathy of the writers for female emancipation, they are to some extent negative role models, serving as a warning to others tempted to ignore social mandates. A woman's possibilities are exposed as limited. Whichever road she takes, her happiness is never guaranteed.

The treatment of men in the works is closely related to the particular role the author assigns to women. They are often less developed as characters, shadowy background figures depicted neither negatively, nor positively. In contrast to the mothers, the fathers in these books are distant but kindly, although more rigid and authoritarian in any conflict between their principles and their parental love. Only in *La Mauvaise Passe* is the father malevolent, but even he is less involved than his wife. As in the works of Diallo, Bâ, and Sow Fall, men become more absorbed by religion as they age.

Male characters as partners are a special group and in some works they are reminiscent of the men in Mariama Bâ's novels. In Ka's first stories, men are a threat to women. In *La Voie du salut*, although Rokhaya's husband has progressive ideas about his daughter's upbringing and education, he gives scant regard to his wife, once the period of romance is over. He forsakes her company for that of his friends and pours scorn on her desires and opinions. Yet he is a benign figure compared with the young men in Rabiatou's life. Her husband's friends are charming to her face, but complain bitterly to Racine about her presence on their outings: "La femme est faite pour rester à la maison" (86) [The wife's place is in the home]. When Racine expresses his astonishment that intellectuals should have such a retrograde mentality, they use the same argument as Ousmane in *Un Chant écarlate*:" Nous n'en sommes pas moins des nègres" (87) [We are still African]. It seems that little has changed with the generations. These young men feel they should not be tied to one woman and with their persistence they seduce Racine away from his wife.

The maid's boyfriend is the villain of *Le Miroir de la vie*. Fatou is immediately deceived by his flattery and eventually yields to his advances, believing his claims of love and promise of marriage. When she tells him she is pregnant, he merely exclaims "pauvre idiote!" (170) [poor fool] and disappears for ever. Fatou's suicide is not unusual. Many young country girls are seduced and abandoned in the city and some kill themselves because they cannot give a name to their child. Fatou is described as "la proie facile d'un individu sans vergogne" (194) [the easy prey of an individual without shame]. Once again Ka exposes the defenselessness of women in their marital and romantic relationships, whether they have a traditional or a modern upbringing.

Mame Seck Mbacke is the only other writer to present such a negative picture of men. In her case studies there are as many male victims as female, yet Mbacke chooses to spotlight Youmané's tragic mistreatment by two white men, called "Dupont" and "Martin." As these names are among the commonest in France, the men are clearly meant to be representative. Mbacke implies that African women should beware of white men and should certainly not marry them and live in France. Yet Thérèse Kuoh-Moukoury in her sociological study, *Les Couples Dominos*, claims that the failure rate in racially mixed marriages is no higher than that in other marriages (184). It may be that because her work in France involved problem cases, Mbacke has a more negative view of the situation than it warrants. In contrast, although Ken Bugul deplores her role as a consumer product for some white men, her experience with them is both positive and negative and is closely related to the lifestyle she freely adopts in Belgium.

In her latest work, Aminata Maïga Ka is no longer so categorical in her presentation of men as partners. Awa's first husband, Tanor, is portrayed as a good man, although he betrays his first wife's hard work and devotion by marrying again and abandoning his first family. The reader even sympathizes with him after his impoverishment and persecution by Awa. Tanor finally understands that Awa cannot be a good wife to him because she does not love him. Furthermore, her first love and second husband, Demba, is the most positive character in the novel. Intelligent and altruistic in his work, faithful and loving in his private life, he is an exemplary model of unselfish dedication to his people and country.

The two most recent novels avoid any accusation of feminine bias by having male protagonists. In *La Mauvaise Passe*, Alioune's representative role as street boy, gang member, drug addict, and alcoholic could not have been filled by a girl. Yet he becomes an outcast because he is a victim, not only of his parents but also of his sisters. Aïcha Diouri chooses as her subject the vulnerability of the male child when abandoned by his mother. In *Mademba*, Khadi Fall's main character has a similar childhood to Alioune, but not because of the neglect of his parents. They unwittingly put him into the hands of an unscrupulous holy man, in search of financial gain through his Coranic pupils. Unlike Alioune, Mademba succeeds in earning an honest living by cleaning shoes. Although not such a flamboyant and fascinating character as his cousin Faatim, his thoughtfulness and decency make the reader identify positively with him, yet without any deep emotional commitment. At one point while in the hospital, he momentarily falls into the role of the stereotypical would-be seducer, but quickly repents of this other self, "ce Mademba-joueur" (130) [that Mademba-player], and abandons the game. Thus, in the latest novels, there is a clear movement away from blanket condemnation of men and an attempt to illuminate the complexities of their responsibilities and aspirations.

Causes of Alienation

In their portrayal of the female condition, these writers seem to be asking the same question: Is the African woman today in a better position than her predecessors? Three factors are shown to be decisive in changing the lives and the mentality of the protagonists: education, the migration from the village to the city and the move from Senegal to

Europe. Although the effects of these changes are not confined to women, and can be equally devastating for men, the authors show that women are especially vulnerable when they leave a traditional environment.

Collier de cheville et *En Votre Nom et au mien* are the only works unequivocally in favor of formal schooling for girls, but only at the elementary level. The other writers are more skeptical about the results of education. In Mbacke's "Youmané l'Africaine exilée," Youmané's father allows her to attend school. She only goes in order to escape housework and soon tires of the effort, entering domestic service to get to the city. Mbacke's opinion of modern education remains unclear. Youmané's sister does not go to school, stays in the village, and is perfectly happy. In *La Voie du salut*, lack of schooling creates a barrier between Rokhaya and her husband and daughter: "Pour n'avoir pas été à l'école des Blancs, son jugement était toujours considéré comme sans valeur" (56) [Because she had not been to the whites' school, her opinions were always considered to be of no value]. In contrast, Rabiatou, a brilliant student, continues her studies in France and eventually becomes a magistrate. Her future husband, Racine, admires her education, independence, and intelligence before they are married, but his initial enlightenment does not prevent him finally abandoning her for a courtesan. Ka shows that education can lead to an important role in public affairs, but it cannot protect a woman in her personal life. For Ken Bugul, what she always refers to as "l'école française" [the French school] plays a dramatic role in her early alienation from society. Rejected by her grandmother because she was the first girl in the family to attend school, Bugul constantly returns to the theme, along with that of the departure of her mother: "La vraie solitude c'était le départ de la mère, l'école française, la mort du père et toujours la solitude" (98). [True loneliness was the mother's departure, the French school, the father's death, and then again loneliness (82)]. Later Ken talks of "l'école française qui allait bouleverser mille mondes et mille croyances" (115) [the French school that was to upset a thousand worlds and a thousand beliefs (98)]. She nostalgically contrasts her life with that of her "twin sister," a relative born on the same day. Ken envies the other girl's lack of schooling and her traditional rural upbringing, even though at the age of puberty she is married to a stranger. Once Ken has begun her western education, she feels estranged from tradition: "J'avais toujours été en dehors des événements de la famille. Les chemins de nos mondes avaient pris des sens différents" (142). [I'd always been on the outside of family events. Our paths had taken different directions (123)]. In her solitude, school becomes the only point of reference, but by the time Ken receives the scholarship to Belgium, she is more interested in continuing her search for her true self than in pursuing her education. Her French schooling, based on the premise of "our ancestors, the Gauls," was a lie. Formal studies have lost their relevance, but Ken cannot eliminate their effects. In contrast to the point of view of Diallo and Bâ, whole-heartedly in favor of schooling for women, this group of writers are generally skeptical about its benefits, or at least aware of the possible disaffection from family and tradition. Their ambivalence is closer to the attitude of Sow Fall in *L'Appel des arènes.*

Another cause of alienation and a potential danger to the young women in these novels is the migration from village to city, a theme also prominent in the novels of Aminata Sow Fall. Ka's Fatou and Mbacke's Youmané come to the city for domestic service. The case of Fatou is typical of that of many girls, migrating during the dry season but returning to the village during the rains. Their home remains in the village, where they often marry and settle down, like Hélène in *Le Revenant*. Yet sometimes these girls cannot return because they fall into disgrace, as do both Fatou and Youmané, and the exile becomes permanent. Youmané is happier in the city and even Fatou feels that her life there, hard as it is, is much easier than her mother's in the village. In reality, the family in the village would starve, were it not for the money Fatou earns. There is no idealization of rural life, ravaged by drought for many years. Nevertheless, the city represents a serious moral danger to naive young women from the country.

Ken's departure from the village takes place because of schooling and for a while she is forced to live in the capital with a westernized older brother and family. Although Bugul shows little interest in social commentary in the manner of Bâ, Sow Fall, or Ka, she reveals her contempt for such African *toubabs*, by emphasizing the coldness of their existence through instruments of separation such as a refrigerator, telephone, floor tiles, cutlery and chairs. In *Le Baobab fou* the village is more than a place. It is a symbol of warmth and light. Identified with the forces of nature, the sun, the sand, and above all the baobab, the village is a protective womb regarded with longing by the narrator. The two prologues, "Préhistoire de Ken" and "Histoire de Ken," describe the creation of the village and at the end the narrator returns to the village and the baobab. As it does in Africa in general, Bugul's baobab represents the positive forces of life: tradition, fertility, continuity, and survival. Witness to the important events of Ken's childhood, it remains the constant companion of her thoughts, but on her return to the village, she discovers that the tree has long been dead. Ken believes that the baobab went mad and died because she did not keep her promise to return. Roger Dorsinville says that she is really referring to her own closeness to madness over the failure of her quest for the meaning of life (150). This interpretation is plausible, considering the close identification between the narrator and the tree. Whatever the exact significance, there is a radiant, delicate beauty in the description of the tree which belies a pessimistic interpretation of its death: "Le soleil veillait le défunt qui était tout en lumière. Les oiseaux portaient le deuil. Les petits papillons blancs et jaunes sillonnaient l'air de leurs ailes lumineuses et tremblantes" (181). [The sun was guarding the dead one as it stood fully lit. The birds were in mourning. The little white and yellow butterflies were fluttering in the air on their luminous and trembling wings (159).] The baobab seems to represent the narrator's life up to this moment. In the last few lines of the book she is saying farewell to that life and welcoming a new and better one: "Sans paroles, je prononçais l'oraison funèbre de ce baobab témoin et complice du départ de la mère, le premier matin d'une aube sans crépuscule" (182) [Wordlessly, I pronounced the eulogy of the baobab tree that had been witness to and accomplice in the mother's departure, the first morning of a dawn without dusk (159)]. The idea of rebirth has already appeared in the text. Just before she left Europe, the mentally and emotionally devastated Ken prayed that God would wipe out her past and give her new life. At the end of her autobiography, her prayer is apparently answered.

The third possible cause of alienation revealed in these books is the move from Senegal to Europe. The theme of the diaspora is a new theme in women's writing, although it has an important place in the books of male writers such as Sembène Ousmane, acknowledging a significant Senegalese presence in Europe. Life in France is treated very briefly in Ka's *La Voie du salut*. Rabiatou has similar impressions to those of Awa in Diallo's *Awa la petite marchande*. The color and warmth of Senegal are contrasted with the greyness and impersonality of Paris. Rabiatou's stay is fortunately temporary and finally beneficial, as she comes to appreciate her African origins and to understand the traditional values of the mother she had previously despised. No longer wishing to become as French as possible, she asks herself: "Comment ce pays, dont les valeurs étaient à l'agonie, pouvait-il prétendre être le modèle de l'Afrique" (59). [How could this country with its dying values claim to be the model for Africa?]. Her treatment by Europeans reveals at best tolerance rather than acceptance, but her experience is not traumatic as she soon returns home.

Mbacke's work is a much stronger indictment of racism in France. Her title, *Le Froid et le piment*, refers to the coldness and the pain of immigrant life in a hostile foreign culture. The case studies in the first half describe the consequences, frequently tragic, of living in France. Although racism is a common theme, the French are not always blamed for the predicament of Africans, often unable to adapt to the new life-style. The briefness of the case studies is supplemented by the two stories. "Un homme de couleur raconte" describes the sordid life in Paris of some black and Arab men, who spend their evenings in bars and their nights with prostitutes, resigned to a marginal existence as the dregs of society. The protagonist, Barry, left his village as a boy to fight in the Algerian war and has never been back. When he wins a large sum of money, he decides to go home, but is murdered and his money stolen before he can leave.

Youmané's problems begin when she leaves her Senegalese employers for a white family. The man repeatedly rapes her and when she finally becomes pregnant at the moment of reaching puberty, throws her out. The birth of a half-white baby is an irreparable dishonor and Youmané can never go back to the village. Several years later she marries a young Frenchman, Gérard, and departs for France. Paris disappoints her with its greyness and indifference and she is faced with the racial prejudice of her parents-in-law, despite their membership of the "Mouvement contre le Racisme." Society in general treats her as a thing and not a person and her husband and even her daughter turn against her: "Elle était seule, vraiment seule. Elle aurait préféré la solitude de la tombe à ce qu'elle endurait" (168) [She was alone, really alone. She would have preferred the solitude of the tomb to what she was enduring]. Finally, when Gérard abandons his family despite the birth of a second child, Youmané turns to prostitution, to work while the children are sleeping. As a result, the children are taken away. Nothing else matters and she welcomes the mortal illness with only one thought on her mind. In a desperate letter she asks her mother to recover the children and take them back to Africa. Youmané had tried to forget her origins and become assimilated into French society, but she always remained a foreigner. In both the case studies and the stories, Mbacke seems to be advising Africans to stay at home, because they will never be accepted as full human beings in Europe.

Also deeply attracted by European culture, Ken Bugul leaves for Belgium in search of her ancestors, but she too discovers the iciness and anonymity experienced by all Africans on arrival. When she looks in a mirror in a wig shop, the truth suddenly dawns: "Oui, j'étais une Noire, une étrangère" (50) [Yes, I was a Black, a Blackwoman, a foreigner

(38)]. Despite her many white friends, Ken feels frustrated because her identification with them is not reciprocated. She encourages the western fascination for Africa, while at the same time being disgusted by it: "Ils me dépouillaient, me vidaient, m'étalaient" (102) [They were stripping me, emptying me out, displaying me (85)]. Alcohol, drugs, and promiscuity are destroying her. The narrator considers herself doubly alienated, first by the colonization of Africa, which made Africans anguished for ever, and second by the ordeal of neocolonialism. At the end of her stay in Europe, Ken is no further in her attempt to establish her identity: "J'avais déménagé de la rue de la Source où la source s'était tarie sans que j'aie pu retourner aux sources" (117). [I moved from the rue de la Source, where the source had dried up my being able to go back to the source (99)]. Yet the peace of the ending in front of the baobab suggests that the narrator has exorcised herself of the European influence. Ken's dilemma is not the same as that of most of the cases described in Mbacke's book, where economic need leads to emigration, nor does she have the same perception of the world as Youmané. Yet both Ken and Youmané have in their own way been seduced by the idea that Europe is the Promised Land. The reality soon uncovers the emptiness of their illusions.

Mademba's cousin, Faatim, also leaves Senegal to study in Paris. She returns a different person, a rebel, particularly against paternal authority, in spite of her previous excellent relations with her father. Nothing more is revealed about Faatim's experience in Europe. Both in terms of her education and her unconventional social views, she is portrayed as an eccentric individual, not as an exemplary case.

General Social Commentary

Education and internal and external migration estrange some of the protagonists from their origins, presenting them with a disconcerting set of new values and customs. Yet this opposition between tradition and progress can appear in many forms, not only in reference to the main characters, but also as general social commentary. Ka treats this conflict most overtly in *La Voie du salut,* inferring the impossibility of deciding categorically between the two. A similarly ambivalent attitude towards the past and the present is evident in *Le Miroir de la vie*, the title itself suggesting a descriptive rather than a prescriptive intention.

Yet Ka also reveals the untenability of some traditions. Like Mariama Bâ, she shows in *Le Miroir de la vie* that young people in the city are no longer prepared to accept the caste system as a basis for marriage. The intended union between the politician's daughter, Ndèye, of aristocratic lineage, and Saliou, the son of the family *griotte*, is considered a horrifying mismatch by both mothers, but there is no reconciling the points of view of the two generations. In the end, after her mother has ruined herself financially, physically, and emotionally in an attempt to prevent the marriage, Ndèye simply escapes the situation by joining her fiancé in France. Caste is not an issue in Ka's latest work but it is a theme in Khadi Fall's *Mademba*. The refusal of Faatim's family of noble origin to sanction her union with the man of *griot* caste she met in France contributes to the failure of her marriage. Being a rebel, she almost marries again, precisely because the prospective husband is of slave caste. Fall's attitude to the caste system is not clear, but Faatim's function as a positive character makes the reader suspect that the author shares her opinion. Another traditional practice condemned by Ka is excision. A three-month-old baby dies as a result of it in a heartrending episode in *La Voie du salut*. In the same work and in *En Votre Nom et au mien*, polygamy is also presented in an unfavorable light, as it is in *Mademba*. In addition, Ka denounces the dowry system in her latest novel. The unrealistically high dowry demanded by Awa's aunts ruin her initial plans for marriage with Demba.

The writers' criticism is also directed at some recent developments in African society, related to urbanization. In *La Mauvaise Passe* and *En Votre Nom et au mien*, drugs are exposed as a scourge in present-day Senegal. In Aïcha Diouri's short novel, drugs are associated with the lives of street children, as is alcohol. Alioune becomes addicted but is cured in the children's home. In Ka's latest work, Awa's brother,

Samba, leaves home for the streets, because he is already a drug addict. His death from an overdose is discovered accidentally by his mother, through a photograph in a newspaper. *Mademba* introduces the theme of street children but not of drugs. The increasing poverty in the countryside is accelerating the process of urbanization and dislocation of an increasing percentage of the population. Although in Diouri's work, Alioune is rehabilitated, Lilyan Kesteloot states in her introduction that such a solution is not possible for the majority of children.

Like Bâ and Sow Fall, the women writers under discussion decry the role of money in modern society and in particular the parasitical nature of the new African elite. The rich women in *Le Miroir de la vie* are particularly guilty in this respect. Ka ridicules their obsession with aping western ways and praises government policies designed to eradicate undesirable customs, such as the spending of huge sums of money on family celebrations and the use of *xeesal.* She hopes that the campaign against corruption will curb the extravagance of the ruling classes. Catherine N'Diaye also has some biting criticisms of what she calls the new rich exploiters and reactionaries (145). They did nothing to bring about Independence, yet profit from preaching nationalism, all the while making their fortunes from the underdevelopment of the country. Constantly mouthing the word "authenticity," they straighten their hair and shop in Paris, contaminating the values of ordinary people with their image of success (145). Khadi Fall shares the negative view of the African elite. At the end of *Mademba,* the narrator recounts a dream in which Faatim's brother, Sidaat, symbolically prostitutes himself to European experts to obtain money, ostensibly for the country but really for himself: "Il était prêt à tout faire pour eux pourvu qu'ils lui accordent les millions demandés" (167) [He was ready to do anything for them, provided that they gave him the millions requested]. In her family, only Faatim has integrity. It is common knowledge that her father's shady dealings as a customs official are the source of his wealth.

The new rich are not the only ones sabotaging the system to their own advantage. Ka, like Sow Fall in *L'Ex-père de la nation,* reveals the decay of medical care in *Le Miroir de la vie*. Hospitals are filthy, flea-ridden, and a source of dangerous contagion because of the widespread corruption, particularly of lower-grade workers. Yet this desire to increase one's income by any means is partly the fault of the government. Since Independence it has failed to provide the mass of the population with its basic needs.

Catherine N'Diaye, probably because of her special situation as an outsider, is more interested in the obvious effects of economic neocolonialism on Senegalese life than the corruption within. She admires the way in which the indigenous culture has sometimes adapted technology to its own needs, as when the transistor radio is used to make funeral announcements: "Que la radio portative vienne au secours des traditions les plus ancrées–au lieu de les anéantir voilà un détournement imprévisible et réjouissant" (80) [That the portable radio comes to the aid of the most firmly rooted traditions–instead of destroying them that is an unexpected and heartening turnabout]. Yet she is profoundly disturbed by what she calls "les rebuts de l'Occident" [western rubbish], the title of one of her essays. She regrets that cheap European merchandise has replaced the products of traditional crafts, but sadly accepts the inevitability of the process. What she really objects to is the way in which the Third World has become the "poubelle des pays riches" (144) [the garbage can of the rich countries] with regard to bad films, worthless literature, and cheap ornaments. The same negative influence is evident in the realm of advertising and in the vulgarization of African art destined for export. Saddest of all to her is the fact that Africans themselves have adopted the aesthetic standards of Europeans and have begun to like "l'art missionnaire." *Gens de sable* thus ends with an example of the destruction of that very spirituality in daily life that is the main subject of the book. Nonetheless, she implies that the underlying African culture is strong enough to survive this new form of colonialism.

In contrast, Ka highlights like Sow Fall, not the commercial influence of the West, but the insidious political interference of some western powers in the internal affairs of African countries. In *Le Miroir de la vie*, the politician's son, Omar, is a member of a group that protests violently against this interference by planting bombs at the entrance of some diplomatic missions "bien connues pour leur appartenance aux forces coloniales et néocoloniales" (148) [well known for belonging to the colonial and neocolonial forces]. These young men object to the assumption that independent African countries can be manipulated with impunity: "Le nègre n'est plus cet enfant qui accepte les diktats des puissances paternalistes qui, en fait, n'oeuvrent que pour leurs propres intérêts" (169) [The negro is no longer the child who accepts the dictates of the paternalistic powers, who, in fact, are only working for their own interests] Both Ka and N'Diaye agree that Independence has not brought an end to the colonizing process. It has simply become more insidious.

Thus the works by other Senegalese women are not radically different in form or content from those by Diallo, Bâ, and Sow Fall. The convergence of interests is not surprising as, although these latest writers are sometimes called the new generation, they are in some cases contemporaries of the others or were writing their books at the same time. Like Diallo, Bâ, and Sow Fall, they are all socially committed to some degree. Likewise, they have chosen to center their writing on their own gender, while being acutely aware of the relevance of social issues to both men and women, especially with regard to cultural conflict. Nevertheless, two opposing tendencies stand out, marking developments with regard to the earlier publications. In the work of Mbacke, Ka, and Diouri there is even greater emphasis on the overtly sociological, while the style and to some extent content of the books by Bugul, Catherine N'Diaye and Khadi Fall reveal a desire to escape that same approach, so characteristic of African literature. In addition, unlike Diallo and Bâ, and in common with Sow Fall, these writers are not convinced that education provides the solution to social problems. Some themes new to women's writing have also appeared: life in the diaspora, the proliferation of the drug problem and the increase in the number of street children.

The works of Bugul and N'Diaye illustrate an attempt to develop an innovative style of writing away from "social realism." Their literary approach is more complex, more personal and less bound by the need to conform to the role of teacher-educator. In the 1985 Magnier interview, Bugul claims to have completed a novel and to be writing a play. In *Ecrivains africains et Identités culturelles–Entretiens*, Pierrette Herzberger-Fofana refers to a second novel at the press: *Rilwan ou la Chute des Nuages* (Dakar: N.E.A.) but I have been unable to locate any other publications under either the name Ken Bugul or Mariétou Mbaye.

The essay form of Catherine N'Diaye's meditations give her the opportunity to overtly express her preoccupation with the present and future state of African literature. In her postscript to *Gens de sable*, she discusses the way in which literature has been repeating itself since Independence and claims it is time that "Third-World" writers stopped being social and political scientists and became artists. She defends her own aesthetic approach by claiming that beauty is inseparable from humanity and declares that art must be subject to aesthetic criteria, not merely be justified in terms of good intentions (157). She deplores the fact that politics finally devour everything else, resulting in acculturation, the absence of quality and the death of good literature (159). Since *Gens de sable*, N'Diaye has written two more books, *La Coquetterie ou la passion du détail* (1987) and *La Gourmandise: Délices d'un péché* (1993). Both exhibit the same eye for detail and talent for expression that make her first book so fascinating, but neither could remotely be classified as African literature.

Of the most recent works, *Mademba* is the most interesting from a literary point of view, because of the framework of the story and because of the skillful intermingling of past and present action, slowly divulging the lives of the two protagonists. Although Khadi Fall undoubtedly has social attitudes, she conveys them subtly through her plot and characters, so that the reader sees Faatim and Mademba as individuals, not merely as representative figures.

VI

Conclusion

Although autobiography plays a role in women's writing from Senegal, Lambrech's statement, referred to in Chapter 1, that it is "the literary genre most chosen by contemporary black African women" (136) does not accurately reflect the works studied. Nor was Guyonneau correct in attaching the label "autobiography" to Mbacke's *Le Froid et le piment* and, as far as can be ascertained, to Adja Ndiaye's *Collier de cheville*. Of the nineteen books discussed, only two are autobiographies: Diallo's *De Tilène au Plateau* and Bugul's *Le Baobab fou*. In addition, Bâ's *Une Si Longue Lettre* is often called an autobiographical novel and Kenneth Harrow, in his article "The Poetics of African Littérature de Témoignage," includes it in his section "Autobiographical littérature de témoignage," along with Diallo and Bugul. Indeed, the rest of the works by Senegalese women could also be encompassed by one of Harrow's categories, either as "social littérature de témoignage," or in the case of *Le Fort maudit*, as "historical littérature de témoignage," because of their concern with identity and cultural validation. Harrow sees testimonial literature as the basic form in Sub-Saharan Africa, reflecting "the conflicts and tensions generated by the confrontations of African and European cultures" (141). He defines this conflict in its most essential aspects as the one between tradition and modernity. This clash between two sets of values is also the basic theme appearing throughout the works by Senegalese women, even by the very absence of modernizing influences, as in *Le Fort maudit*. Thus women's writing is solidly anchored in the literary conventions established by African men. Like their male counterparts, the women novelists reject art for art's sake and align themselves fully with social commitment.

The Female Protagonists in the Novels under Study

Nevertheless, there is a major difference between male and female writing. In the texts by women, cultural conflict is almost always related to the female condition, even if other aspects of the same problematic are also treated. This common element exists despite the differing attitudes of women novelists from Senegal towards their role as writers. Female characters always play a primary role. Even where the main character is male, there is a case to be made for a female being the dynamic force in the plot. In every novel except *La Mauvaise Passe,* it can be argued that the function of women is more significant than that of men. This prominence is in stark contrast to male writing, where, with a few notable exceptions, women generally play a secondary role.

In general, what sort of heroines or female protagonists have the women novelists created? Sunday Anozie in his *Sociologie du Roman Africain* categorizes three types of heroes in African novels by men: the hero "de détermination traditionnelle," who accepts traditional values, the hero "de détermination intro-active," who questions the traditional world and the hero "de détermination extro-active," who rejects the traditional world with all its values. Because the conflict between tradition and progress is the basic theme of Senegalese women's writing, Anozie's categories are a useful point of departure in an analysis of the female protagonists, enabling us to examine the novelists in terms of this fundamental dialectic.

Apart from Diallo's two historical works, the novels by women are all set either in the period just preceding Independence or in post-Independence Senegal. This time of transition, of profound social change and uncertainty, is revealed in the attitudes of the main characters and also in their situation as urban dwellers, although a number came originally from the country. The result is that there are few heroines "de détermination traditionnelle." The most obvious is Thiane in *Le Fort maudit,* where traditional Africa and Islam are fused in an idealized portrayal of precolonial life, contrasted only with the barbarity of pagan Baol. Thiane, as a positive representative of the traditional feminine condition, is fully integrated into her world, and only rebels against its aggressors. Yet the other protagonists "de détermination traditionnelle" are perhaps more significant, because the works in which they appear are set in modern times. Rokhaya, the mother in Ka's *La Voie du salut*, never questions the values acquired during her village upbringing, but she shares the role of main character with her progressive daughter, Rabiatou, to whom she is a foil. Rokhaya is a victim. She desires happiness in an active relationship with her husband and daughter, but she is reduced to a passive role, marginalized by her lack of schooling. The maid, Fatou, in Ka's *Le Miroir de la vie* does not challenge traditional values either. She is also a victim. Despite her employment in an urbanized, westernized family from the new-rich political elite, her life offers little choice and she remains excluded from the benefits of both traditional life and modernization. Both Rokhaya and Fatou exemplify the powerlessness of women denied a place in the modern world.

Tante Lika in *Collier de cheville* and Sow Fall's Salla Niang in *La Grève des Bàttu* could also be described as "de détermination traditionnelle." Unlike Fatou and Rokhaya, these two women are not victims. Salla Niang comes from the country, but refuses to be confined to a passive role. Obliged through poverty to move to the city, she still holds traditional communal values, but feels compelled to survive through the urban activity of begging. She highlights the predicament of the modern adherent to tradition outside the village environment. Exposure to progress is inevitable and some form of adaptation essential. At the same time, Salla Niang's achievements reveal the possibility of enacting positive social change.

The only female protagonist unequivocally belonging to Anozie's category "de détermination intro-active" is Fary in Diallo's *La Princesse de Tiali*. On the surface a submissive wife in a traditional historical context, she refuses to accept the constraints of the caste system and triumphs. Yet other aspects of her revolt are more closely related to the defence and spread of Islam than to the undermining of established norms. Yama in Sow *Fall's Le Revenant* could also be described as "de détermination intro-active." She questions traditions, but only in so far as they create an obstacle to her own ambitions. She rejects caste in favor of money because she has wealth without lineage. Yama's attitudes are based not on ideals but on pragmatic self-interest, reflecting the prevailing mores of the new urban society as Sow Fall sees it. Other women remain profoundly attached to some aspects of tradition, but question or reject customs conflicting with their present status or opinions. Safi in *De Tilène au Plateau*, Diallo's adolescent heroine, Awa, and Ka's Awa in *En Votre Nom et au mien* all query traditional limitations on the freedom of the individual, particularly of women, and they believe in the power of education to bring about beneficial social change, but they do not revolt in any radical way against the constraints imposed on them by their essentially conservative families. Bâ's Ramatoulaye displays a similar point of view. Although in favor of women's liberation and a passionate believer in the formal knowledge acquired through books, she finds herself unable to violate the traditional code of behavior with regard to marriage.

A number of main characters could be described as "de détermination extro-active" in their rejection of traditional values, but they do not all fit neatly into the same schema. Mbacke's Yamané spurns the restrictions for women of rural life and chooses to move to the city, but then loses control of her destiny, being carried along by events rather than shaping them herself. Even her move to France, motivated partly by her illusions about metropolitan life, appears to be more closely tied to her desire for love and security than to a conscious choice of values or life-style. Yandé, Madiama's second wife in *L'Ex-père de la nation,* changes from being "de détermination traditionnelle" to "de détermination extro-active." Brought up in rural Senegal, she is the stereotypical victimized wife until her violent mutiny against her first husband's cruelty. A social outcast until her marriage to Madiama, she creates a new world, establishing herself as a power center in a web of political intrigue. Yet her situation is always precarious and even she cannot prevail against the neocolonial machinations from abroad.

Ka's Rabiatou, Sow Fall's Diattou and Khadi Fall's Faatim are a different group "de détermination extro-active." Considering themselves progressive, educated young women, they consciously reject the past and believe they can lead their lives as individuals without constant reference to collective constraints. Diattou is an extreme example. She has a pathological distaste for community values and African tradition. Ken Bugul is a more complex case. Although she leaves Senegal to create an existence for herself that is profoundly individualistic and alien to her origins, she feels her European education and lack of family affection have cheated her of the stability of village life. At the end of *Le Baobab fou*, she turns back to the past and chooses the village as the solution to her trauma.

Thus the protagonists of the novels studied, with the exception of Diattou, are torn to a greater or lesser degree between a feeling of regret for the passing of those aspects of traditional life they consider positive and the desire to fulfil their own personal needs through the prerogative of choice not available in a traditional context. This ambivalence can be traced through most of the works, and there is no clear evolution in preference from the collective to the individualistic. Yet one protagonist stands apart from the others and a new category could be created for her that I would like to call "de détermination inter-active." Sow Fall's Naarou in *Le Jujubier du patriarche* represents a harmonious reconciliation between the value systems of the past and the present. She experiences no conflict between her strong sense of individual freedom and worth and her affiliation with the past and the clan through the epic poem. An educated woman without complexes, Naarou personifies the positive aspects of both cultures while illustrating the timeless necessity for love and forgiveness.

The Image of Women in Writing by African Men

A comparison between male and female writers from Africa necessitates a brief examination of the image of women in writing by men. Critical work on male writing constantly emphasizes the stereotypical depiction of women by men. The most defining role for women in African society is that of mother. The theme of the sacred nature of motherhood and its exaltation into the symbol of Mother Africa was particularly important in the Negritude movement as an element of protest against colonialism, well-known through the poetry of Léopold Senghor. The portrait of the devoted mother is also to be found in novels. In her article "La promotion féminine à travers les romans africains," Arlette Chemain-Degrange beautifully describes these idealized women as: "Génitrices incarnant la bonté et le dévouement, liées aux symboles de la prospérité et de la fécondité chtonienne, à l'idée de la profusion alimentaire et aux satisfactions du stade oral" (36). [Female reproducers incarnating goodness and devotion, linked to the symbols of prosperity and chtonian fecundity, to the idea of alimentary profusion and to the satisfactions of the oral stage].

The mother can also symbolize suffering, in a mythical sense in poetry, but also in a brutally realistic way in novels such as those by the Cameroonians, Mongo Beti and Ferdinand Oyono. Yet, as Chemain-Degrange herself indicates in "L'Image de la 'Mère dévorante'," in African literature there is also the parallel opposing image of aggressive femininity inherited from the character of the wicked stepmother in the folk-tales. Both images of the mother-as-saint and the mother-as-monster are more closely related to myth, or at least to stereotype, than to reality, but they do reveal the ambivalent attitude of male writers towards the mother figure as simultaneously oppressed and oppressive.

The second female role of importance is that of wife. Both Sonia Lee (60) and Mohamadou Kane (382) affirm that all the novelists they studied, whatever their political and social views, present women in a position of inferiority in traditional marriage. This is not only the case in novels from predominantly Islamic countries, but is also true in the Cameroonian novels, where the characters practice either Christianity or traditional religion.

The third type of woman depicted in novels is the unmarried girl or "free" woman. Lee claims that the figure of the young woman is the most fascinating to male authors because she represents greater diversity as well as incarnating most clearly the dilemma of women in today's world (149). In West African literature in English, these women are often "loose" types (Mutiso 51). Sexually free women also exist in the novels of Oyono and Beti, but in predominantly Moslem countries, the emphasis in literature is on the liberation of women, if it exists, in a sense other than sexual. Nevertheless, Chemain-Degrange in her article "Emancipation féminine et littérature négro-africaine (poésie et roman)" highlights the reluctance of male writers, even progressive ones like Sembène Ousmane, to depict the emancipation of women in a professional sense, either because they are afraid of female rivalry or because of a deeper, irrational fear of castration by the female figure (20). Kenneth Little in *The Sociology of Urban Women's Image in African Literature* also comments on the absence in West African anglophone literature of women with professional or public authority.

Lee stresses that male writers are sympathetic towards the position of women, both because of their relationship with their mother and because of their western-style education. Yet Oladele Taiwo in his *Female Novelists of Modern Africa* claims that the female image in male writing is distasteful to women because men have presented women in a position of inferiority, even though, in his opinion, this is a true reflection of the social reality (11). Roseann Bell does not agree that literary depiction is true to life. With reference to books in English, she creates her own categories of women in male writing and calls them earth mother, loyal door-mat wife, concubine and high-life floozy, asserting that they reproduce male prejudices rather than mirror society (491). Despite the controversy about the accuracy of the portrayal of women, most writers on African literature agree that female characters in male writing lack psychological depth. They do not emerge as individuals, but remain confined and defined by their role as mother, wife, or single woman.

The Image of Men in Senegalese Novels by Women

If male writers are often accused of creating female stereotypes, can the same accusation be leveled at women writers in their depiction of men? In reference to the novels under study, with the exception of Aminata Sow Fall's male protagonists, I think it can. Clear patterns stand out in an analysis based on the parallel categories of father, husband, and single man. In most of the novels, the father remains a distant symbolic presence, whether he is kindly or tyrannical. He spends most of his time outside the home, either at work or at the mosque, depending on his age, so that the mother is left to deal with family matters, of which the father is often ignorant. Only in Diallo's work is the father a vital force, comparable to that of the mother in male writing. It could be claimed that the widespread typecasting of the father is a precise image of social reality, appearing also in novels by men, because children have a more intimate relationship with their mother than with their father. At the same time, the social aims of the writers are revealed in the relegation of the father to the background. The cultural conflict at the heart of the Senegalese novel by women, being integrally related to the female condition, is exposed more meaningfully through a comparison with the mother than with the father.

Husbands too remain undeveloped characters in most of the novels, except for Mour in *La Grève des Bàttu*. Yet even he is seen in depth only with regard to his obsession with the vice-presidency. In the other novels, a great variety of husbands are portrayed, depending on the attitude to marriage of the writer in question. In Diallo's works, the husband is a benign figure, presumably because of the influence of Diallo's own father and possibly of her husband. In Bâ's novels and Ka's stories, husbands are weak, unfaithful, and the source of their wives' unhappiness, because both authors aim to denounce the negative marital role of Senegalese men. In Ka's last novel, however, she tempers this harsh image by creating the model partner, Demba Dieng. In the rest of the works, husbands are cast in both a positive and negative light, inferring that marital behavior depends on the ideas and character of the individual man.

Young unmarried men have even less of a role than the father and husband. Except for the protagonists Ousmane in *Un Chant écarlate* and Bakar in *Le Revenant*, more important anyway as husbands, single men are hardly more than a fleeting presence, if they exist at all in the novels. The exception is Mademba. He is a fully rounded character seen from the inside. Young men are usually depicted in their relationship with a girl and may be either positive or negative, depending on their attitude to women. Only Adji Arame's son in *Le Miroir de la vie* is shown otherwise, the focus being on his militant left-wing activity against neocolonialism.

Thus, both male and female writers tend to present the other gender either superficially or from a psychologically limited angle. In both bodies of literature, the defining roles of secondary gender characters are derived from their relationship with the dominant gender.

The Female Condition in Senegalese Novels by Women

Examining the full spectrum of female characters in the Senegalese novels and not just the protagonists, one is struck by the great variety of both positive and negative models. Nevertheless, a number of types can be distinguished, although many individuals fit into more than one category, The mother is an important character, but she is not mythologized and she is not an obsession. In general, she is committed to her offspring, whatever happens, and sometimes she is oppressed. Another recurring figure is the grandmother/mother as friend or accomplice, although she may be a respected matriarch, too. Representatives of Chemain-Degrange's "mère dévorante" are also a common occurrence, either as mother or as mother-in-law.

Yet, despite the importance of her emotive role in the family, the mother in the Senegalese novels usually has a more significant contrastive function in relation to the younger generation, particularly to her daughter. She illustrates a conservative mentality with its acceptance of an imposed life-style, while the daughter represents the modern woman refusing to accept traditional limitations on her freedom of action. The result is conflict, even if the relationship is good. This contrasting viewpoint about the female condition in an essentially harmonious relationship appears in *Une Si Longue Lettre*, *La Grève des Bàttu*, *L'Ex-père de la nation*, *Le Jujubier du patriarche*, *La Voie du salut* and *En Votre Nom et au mien*. More rarely, the bond between mother and child is profoundly disturbed by the difference in mentality, leading to a breakdown of the relationship, as with Adji Arame and Ndeye in *Le Miroir de la vie* and Tante NGoone and Faatim in *Mademba*. Diattou and her son Nalla in *L'Appel des arènes* represent a reversal of the norm. He wishes to reestablish his links with tradition, while she totally rejects the past.

Although cultural conflict is often presented as a generation variance between mother and daughter, it may exist as an internal struggle within the young woman herself, as in the case of Ken Bugul and in a less self-conscious way in those of Ka's Awa and Mbacke's Youmané. Generally, however, the young woman does not incorporate conflict. She is either traditional (Nabou in *Une Si Longue Lettre* and Ouleymatou in *Un Chant écarlate*) or modern (Daba in *Une Si Longue Lettre*, Raabi and Sine in *La Grève des Bàttu*, Nafi in *L'Ex-père de la nation*, Rabiatou in *La Voie du salut* and Faatim in *Mademba*.) Furthermore, in Bâ's writing a male character, Ousmane, is the clearest example of cultural conflict within the individual, and in her first novel the mature married woman, Ramatoulaye, most embodies the dialectic between tradition and progress. It is a mistake to be too categorical with regard to such divisions. Because of the nature of modern Senegalese society, almost all the characters experience cultural conflict to some degree.

The woman as wife is most notable in the novels of Bâ and Ka because of their interest in the couple relationship, and is also prominent in Khadi Fall's *Mademba* and in Mbacke's "Youmané l'Africaine exilée." But in the writing of Diallo and Bugul, all the protagonists, except Fary in the second half of *La Princesse de Tiali*, are young unmarried women and, even if the woman as wife is influential, she remains a secondary figure. In the novels of Aminata Sow Fall, the main female characters are all married, but their marital status is irrelevant in comparison with their personal attributes. Other married women in Sow Fall's work reveal how marital experience can vary widely from one woman to another. The authors thus concentrate on the particular aspect of a woman's existence most interesting to them as social commentators. Generally speaking, they are preoccupied with the personal development of the individual woman and particularly with the element of choice in her life, rather than with one exclusive role.

This emphasis on the inner resources of the woman, on her self-confidence and values, perhaps explains why so little attention is paid to her professional development. In her 1974 article, Chemain-Degrange laments the absence of francophone women writers, convinced they would depict a realistic evolution in the professional status and activity of women. Yet, although a good number of the main female characters in the Senegalese novels by women are professionals and others are students, this aspect of their lives is mostly mentioned but not shown. Those authors who choose educated women as main characters (and Aminata Sow Fall is a notable exception here, except for Diattou) prefer to expose the ambiguities of social transition through human relationships outside the work context, perhaps reflecting a view that the private rather than the public role of women is more instrumental in eventual change.

This concurs with Lloyd Brown's analysis of anglophone writers in *Women Writers in Black Africa.* He says that they advocate personal growth before social transformation, emphasizing self-help and individual initiative (180). As would be expected, writing by women in English has much in common with that in French. All the commentators on anglophone literature point out the greater psychological depth in the characterization of women by women, treated as people first and secondarily in terms of their familial or maternal status. Dealing with the whole body of francophone female writing, both Jean-Marie Volet in his article and Kembe Milolo in her book stress the prominence of the themes of female self-discovery and self-affirmation. A female voice can therefore be discerned in the Senegalese novels with much in common with that in other African novels by women in both English and French. This voice not only centers on the special situation of women. It also stresses the search for the feminine self, that is, for an identity in which women reconcile the opposing forces within and without.

If a clear distinction can be made between Senegalese and other female writing, it is associated with religion. Volet's focus on the theme of the supernatural spirit world in female francophone literature is not applicable to the Senegalese novels. Senegal is the only Islamic country in Black Africa to have produced a body of literature by women. All the women writers in this study appear to be profoundly attached to Islam. Extreme reliance on superstitious practices is satirized and the hypocritical use of Islam as an instrument of male domination is condemned in a number of novels, but a true relationship with God through Islam is either assumed or openly promoted throughout. The religious influence goes even further. Because of the Islamic accent on sexual modesty and chastity, carnal relationships do not play the same significant role in Senegalese novels as they do in the novels of writers from non-Islamic countries, where sexual mores are less rigid and prostitution is an important theme.

The gender bias discernable in the Senegalese novels is the product of the authors' preoccupations, as well as a reflection of their own life experience. Although these women are writing because they have something to say to everyone about contemporary Senegalese society and about their identity as Black Africans in a world threatened by western economic and cultural domination, they are sending a special message to and about women. Within their wider objective, they wish to illuminate the female condition in all its aspects, particularly with regard to a harmonious reconciliation between certain traditional moral and communal values and the emancipation of the individual woman.

In this aspiration women suffer a double conflict, non-existent for men. For the latter, it is simply a question of an opposition between tradition and modernity. Yet tradition sometimes conflicts directly with female emancipation, because it has often been oppressive to women, especially in the marital situation, where they have been simply regarded as property. Senegalese women writers do not resolve this conflict. They show that each man and woman must reflect on the identity crisis and search for an appropriate solution. Yet they reveal that a profound change in the relationship between men and women is central to any process of modernization. They believe in marriage based on free choice and love, although they recognize that these initial conditions are no guarantee of success. They condemn polygamy, not on the practical grounds that it is no longer feasible in a modern urban environment, but rather because they see it as a betrayal of the trust and love in a couple relationship, the ideal they advocate. They affirm the right of women to happiness and avoid wholesale idealization of the past, because of the restrictions on the life of women. Rather they concentrate on the aspects of traditional life they regard as positive.

Despite the fact that Senegalese women writers support a form of individualism generally considered impossible for women in traditional society, they plainly advocate an African individualism, firmly rooted in cultural and social identity. They reject the type of individualism western feminists sometimes promote, in terms of self-identity only slightly influenced by society and culture, because of the relativity of values in the West and the fact that identity is closely tied to the competitive idea of personal gain and personal ambition. Whereas western feminism is attempting to create a feminist set of values, Senegalese women writers are trying to reconcile traditional moral values with freedom of choice. They see themselves as less antagonistic to men than western feminists. The central importance of motherhood and the firm belief in the division of gender roles leads African women to look for a new form of partnership with men. There is no questioning of the role of mother or of the sexuality of women, nor of marriage as a basic and desirable condition. As Filomina Steady asserts in *The Black Woman Cross-Culturally*: "We believe that we can be emancipated without being castrated; that we can strive for equality and still remain female" (32).

Notwithstanding the degree or type of feminism that each one of the Senegalese women writers upholds, they have all chosen the art form of the novel as their means of expression. Even if the literary quality and artistic integrity of the works under study is not uniform, one can say that there is a striving throughout for congruity of form and content. Aesthetic considerations are present in all the works. The human dilemma these writers have to confront necessarily involves the cultural and the feminine, as well as a dialectic with western values and artistic forms. Naturally, criticism is directed at them because of this very dilemma. That is, some Westerners, given current aesthetic theories and fashions, tend to decry their art as too concerned with social values and lacking in aesthetic audacity. Yet, given that this literature is being produced within the context of decolonization, within a turmoil of values and an obvious identity crisis, one can hardly expect a novel from Africa that ignores the very reality from which it emerges. First and foremost, as can be seen from the works themselves, the aim of the writers is to communicate with a readership not confined to western critics, but including the greatest possible audience in their own country. Narrative sophistication in the pursuit of aesthetic originality for its own sake would inevitably impede this communication. This is a quandary faced by African literature as a whole, not only African literature by women.

Notes

1. Ndèye Nianga Mbaye, "Le domicile conjugal" and Mame Seck, "Mame Touba."

2. Sylvie Bokoko, "Mafouaou" and Marie-Rose Turpin, "HLM - P."

3. My analyses of the Senegalese novels are based on the French texts. If one page reference only is given to support a comment, it is to the French text.

4. All English translations of quotations from *De Tilène au Plateau* are from the published translation by Dorothy S. Blair *A Dakar Childhood*. Harlow, Essex: Longman, 1982.

5. Translations of quotations from *Le Fort maudit* are my own.

6. Translations of quotations from *Awa la petite marchande* are my own.

7. Translations of quotations from *La Princesse de Tiali* are taken from the published translation by Ann Woollcombe, *Fary, Princess of Tiali*. Washington D.C.: Three Continents Press, 1987.

8. All English translations of quotations from *Une Si Longue Lettre* are taken from the published translation by Modupé Bodé-Thomas, *So Long a Letter*. London: Heinemann, 1981.

9. Unless otherwise stated, all English translations of quotations from *Un Chant écarlate* are taken from the published translation by Dorothy S. Blair, *Scarlet Song*. Harlow, Essex: Longman, 1985.

10. In my opinion this is a mistranslation. I would translate it as: "*Unique* instrument . . . "

11. Quoted by Mohammad A. Rauf. *Islam: Creed and Worship*. Washington D. C.: The Islamic Center, 1974, p. 107.

12. All translations of quotations from Sow Fall's novels are mine unless otherwise stated.

13. Translations of quotations from *La Grève des Bàttu* are taken from the published translation by Dorothy S. Blair, *The Beggars' Strike*. Harlow, Essex: Longman, 1981.

14. All translations of quotations from *Le Baobab fou* are from the published translation by Marjolijn de Jager, *The abandoned Baobab*. Chicago: Lawrence Hill Books, 1991.

Bibliography

Primary Literary Texts

Bâ, Mariama. *Un Chant écarlate*. Dakar: Les Nouvelles Editions Africaines, 1981.

___. *Scarlet Song*. Translated by Dorothy S. Blair. Harlow, Essex: Longman, 1985.

___. *Une Si Longue Lettre*. Dakar: Les Nouvelles Editions Africaines, 1979.

___. *So Long a Letter*. Translated by Modupé Bodé-Thomas. London: Heinemann, 1981.

Bugul, Ken. *Le Baobab fou*. Dakar: Les Nouvelles Editions Africaines, 1982.

___. *The Abandoned Baobab*. Translated by Marjolijn de Jager. Brooklyn, New York: Lawrence Hill Books, 1991.

Diallo, Nafissatou. *Awa la petite marchande*. Dakar: Les Nouvelles Editions Africaines, 1981.

___. *De Tilène au Plateau*. Dakar: Les Nouvelles Editions Africaines, 1975.

___. *A Dakar Childhood*. Translated by Dorothy S. Blair. Harlow, Essex: Longman, 1982.

___. *Le Fort maudit*. Paris: Hatier, 1980.

___. *La Princesse de Tiali*. Dakar: Les Nouvelles Editions Africaines, 1987.

___. *Fary, Princess of Tiali*. Translated by Anne Woollcombe. Washington, D. C.: Three Continents Press, 1987.

Diouri, Aïcha. *La Mauvaise Passe*. Dakar: Khoudia

Fall, Khadi. *Mademba*. Paris: L'Harmattan, 1989.

Ka, Aminata Maïga. *La Voie du salut suivi de Le Miroir de la vie*. Paris: Présence Africaine, 1985.

___. *En Votre Nom et au mien*. Abidjan: Les Nouvelles Editions Africaines, 1989.

Mbacke, Mame Seck. *Le Froid et le piment*. Dakar: Les Nouvelles Editions Africaines, 1983.

Ndiaye, Adja Ndeye. *Collier de cheville*. Dakar: Les Nouvelles Editions Africaines, 1983.

N'Diaye, Catherine. *Gens de sable*. Paris: P.O.L., 1984.

Sow Fall, Aminata. *L'Appel des arènes*. Dakar: Les Nouvelles Editions Africaines, 1982.

___. *L'Ex-père de la nation*. Paris: L'Harmattan, 1987.

___. "The Former Father of the Nation." Translated in part by William Hemminger. *Southern Humanities Review* 26 (Fall 1992):313-348.

___. *La Grève des Bàttu.* Dakar: Les Nouvelles Editions Africaines, 1979.

___. *The Beggars' Strike.* Translated by Dorothy S. Blair. Harlow, Essex: Longman, 1981.

___. *Le Jujubier du patriarche.* Dakar: Khoudia, 1993.

___. *Le Revenant.* Dakar: Les Nouvelles Editions Africaines, 1976.

Secondary Literary Texts

Adiaffi, Anne-Marie. *Une Vie hypothéquée.* Abidjan: Les Nouvelles Editions Africaines, 1984.

Aidoo, Christina Ama Ata. *The Dilemma of a Ghost.* Ikeja: Longman (Nigeria) Limited, 1965.

Badian, Seydou. *Noces sacrées.* Paris: Présence Africaine, 1977.

___. *Sous l'orage.* Paris: Présence Africaine, 1963.

Bambote, Makombo. *Nouvelles de Bangui.* Montréal: Les Presses de l'Université de Montréal, 1980.

Bebey, Francis. *Le Fils d'Agatha Moudio.* Yaoundé: Editions C.L.E., 9th. edition 1982.

Beti, Mongo. *Mission terminée*. Paris: Corréa-Buchet-Chastel, 1957.

___. *Le Pauvre Christ de Bomba*. Paris: Laffont, 1956. Paris: Présence Africaine, 1976.

Beti, Mongo (under the pseudonym of Eza Boto). *Ville Cruelle*. Paris: Editions Africaines, 1954. Paris: Présence Africaine, 1971.

Beyala, Calixthe. *C'est le soleil qui m'a brûlée*. Paris: Stock, 1987.

Bhély-Quenum, Olympe. *Un Piège sans fin*. Paris: Stock, 1960. Paris: Présence Africaine, 1978.

Bokoko, Sylvie. "Mafouaou." *Trois Nouvelles*. Dakar: Les Nouvelles Editions Africaines, 1982.

Casanova, Marie. *Lat Dior: Le Dernier Souverain du Cayor*. Paris: A.B.C, Dakar: Les Nouvelles Editions Africaines, 1976.

Dadié, Bernard. *Un Nègre à Paris*. Paris: Présence Africaine, 1959.

Dem, Tidiane. *Masséni*. Dakar-Abidajan: Les Nouvelles Editions Africaines, 1977.

Dia, Malick. *L'Impossible Compromis*. Abidjan: Les Nouvelles Editions Africaines, 1979.

Diakhaté, Lamine. *Prisonnier du regard*. Dakar: Les Nouvelles Editions Africaines, 1975.

Diop, Birago. *Les Contes d'Amadou-Koumba*. Paris: Fasquelle, 1947. Paris: Présence Africaine, 1961.

Diop, Boubacar Boris. *Les Tambours de la mémoire*. Paris: L'Harmattan, 1990.

Dooh-Bunya, Lydie. *La Brise du jour*. Yaoundé: Editions CLE, 1977.

Emecheta, Buchi. *The Bride Price*. London: Allison and Busby Limited, 1976.

___. *Destination Biafra*. London: Allison and Busby, 1982.

___. *In the Ditch*. London: Allison and Busby Limited, 1972.

___. *The Rape of Shavi*. New York: George Braziller, Inc., 1985

___. *The Slave Girl*. New York: George Braziller, Inc., 1977.

Ewandé, Daniel. *Vive le Président*. Paris: Albin Michel, 1968.

Fall, Malick. *La Plaie*. Paris: Albin Michel, 1967.

Fantouré, Alioum. *Le Cercle des Tropiques*. Paris: Présence Africaine, 1972.

Faye, N. G. M. *Le Débrouillard*. Paris: Gallimard, 1964.

Hazoumé, Paul. *Doguicimi*. 2nd ed. 1938. Paris: G.P. Maisonneuve et Larose, 1978.

Head, Bessie. *A Question of Power*. New York: Pantheon Books, 1973.

___. *When Rain Clouds Gather*. New York: Simon and Schuster, 1968.

Jabavu, Noni. *Drawn in Colour*. London: John Murray, 1960.

Juminer, Bertène. *Les Héritiers de la Presqu'ile*. Paris: Présence Africaine, 1979.

Ka, Abdou Anta. *Mal*. Dakar: Les Nouvelles Editions Africaines, 1975.

Kalonji, Christine. *Dernière Genèse*. Paris: Saint-Germain-des-Prés, 1975.

Kane, Cheikh Hamidou. *L'Aventure ambiguë*. Paris: René Juillard, 1961. Paris: 10/18, 1971.

Kaya, Simone. *Les Danseuses d'Impe-Eya. Jeunes filles à Abidjan*. Abidjan: INADES, 1976.

Keita, Aoua. *Femme d'Afrique*. Paris: Présence Africaine, 1975.

Klein, Pierre, ed. *Anthologie de la nouvelle sénégalaise (1970-1977)* Dakar: Les Nouvelles Editions Africaines, 1978.

Kourouma, Ahmadou. *Les Soleils des indépendances*. Montreal: Les Presses de l'Université de Montréal, 1968. Paris: Editions du Seuil, 1970.

Laye, Camara. *L'Enfant noir*. Paris: Plon, 1953.

___. *Le Regard du roi*. Paris: Plon, 1954.

Lopes, Henri. *Le Pleurer-rire*. Paris: Présence Africaine, 1982.

Ly, Ibrahima. *Toiles d'araignées*. Paris: L'Harmattan, 1982.

Mbaye D'Erneville, Annette. *La Bague de cuivre et d'argent*. Dakar: Les Nouvelles Editions Africaines, 1983.

___. *Le Noël du vieux chasseur*. Dakar: Les Nouvelles Editions Africaines, 1983.

Mbengue, Mamadou Seyni. *Le Royaume de sable*. Dakar: Les Nouvelles Editions Africaines, 1975.

Mweya, Elisabeth Françoise Tol'ande. *Ahata* and *Le Récit d'une damnée*. Kinshasa: Editions Bobiso, 1977.

Ndao, Cheikh Aliou. *Buur Tilleen*. Paris: Présence Africaine, 1972.

___. *Le Marabout de la sécheresse*. Dakar: Les Nouvelles Editions Africaines, 1979.

N'Daye, Catherine. *La Coquetterie ou la passion du détail*. Paris: Editions Autrement, 1987.

___. *La Gourmandise: Délices d'un péché*. Paris: Editions Autrement, 1993.

Ndiaye, Sada Weïnde. *La Fille des eaux*. Dakar: Les Nouvelles Editions Africaines, 1975.

Ndiaye, Sada Weïnde Hubert. *Le Retour de l'aïeul*. Dakar: Chez l'auteur, 1972.

Nokan, Charles. *Violent était le vent*. Paris: Présence Africaine, 1966.

Nwapa, Flora. *Efuru*. London: Heinemann, 1966.

Ogot, Grace. *The Promised Land*. Nairobi: East African Publishing House, 1966.

Ouologuem, Yambo. *Le Devoir de violence*. Paris: Editions du Seuil, 1968.

Oyono, Ferdinand. *Chemin d'Europe*. Paris: Julliard, 1960.

___. *Une Vie de boy*. Paris: Julliard, 1956.

___. *Le Vieux Nègre et la médaille*. Paris: Julliard, 1956.

Sadji, Abdoulaye. *Maïmouna*. Paris: Présence Africaine, 1958.

___. *Nini, Mulâtresse du Sénégal*. Paris: Présence Africaine, Special Number, "Trois Ecrivains Noirs", 1954. Paris: Présence Africaine, 1965.

Sall, Ibrahima. *Les Routiers de chimères*. Dakar: Les Nouvelles Editions Africaines, 1982.

Samb, Amar. *Matraqué par le destin*. Dakar: Les Nouvelles Editions Africaines, 1973.

Sangaré, Moussa Ly. *Sourd-muet je demande la parole*. Dakar: Les Nouvelles Editions Africaines, 1978.

Sembène, Ousmane. *Les Bouts de bois de Dieu*. Paris: Le Livre Contemporain, 1960.

___. *Le Dernier de l'empire*. Paris: L'Harmattan, 1981.

___. *L'Harmattan*. Paris: Présence Africaine, 1964.

___. *Niiwam suivi de Taaw*. Paris: Présence Africaine 1987.

___. *O Pays mon beau peuple*. Paris: Amiot-Dumont, 1957.

___. *Vehi-Ciosane suivi du Mandat*. Paris: Présence Africaine, 1966.

___. *Voltaïque*. Paris: Présence Africaine, 1962.

___. *Xala*. Paris: Présence Africaine, 1973.

Socé, Ousmane. *Karim*. Paris: Impr. M. Puyfourcat, 1935. Paris: Nouvelles Editions Latines, 1948.

Turpin, Marie-Rose. "H.L.M./P" in *Trois Nouvelle*s. Dakar: Les Nouvelles Editions Africaines, 1982.

Warner-Vieyra, Miriam. *Juletane*. Paris: Présence Africaine, 1982.

Critical Works

Abanime, Emeka. Review of *Une Si Longue Lettre* and *La Grève des Bàttus*. *World Literature Today* 54.2 (1980): 327.

Achiriga, Jingiri J. *La Revolte des romanciers noirs de langue francaise*. Sherbrooke, Quebec: Naaman, 1973.

Aire, Victor O. Review of *Une Si Longue Lettre*. *Canadian Journal of African Studies* 16 (1982): 636-37.

Ajala, John D. *"The Beggars' Strike*: Aminata Sow Fall as a Spokeswoman for the Underprivileged." *C.L.A. Journal* 34.2 (December 1990): 137-152.

Ajayi, J. F. Ade, and Michael Crowder, eds. *History of West Africa.* 2nd ed. Vol. 2. New York: Columbia University Press, 1976. 2 vols.

Anonymous. "Prize for Publishing." *West Africa* no. 3281, 9 June 1980: 1013-14.

Anonymous. Review of *Le Baobab fou. Jeune Afrique Magazine* 2 (February 1984): 72.

Anozie, Sunday. *Sociologie du roman africain.* Paris: Aubier-Montaigne, 1970.

Arnold, Stephen, ed. *African Literature Studies: The Present State/ L'Etat present.* Washington, D.C.: Three Continents Press, 1985.

Atlas International du Sénégal. Paris: Institut Géographique National, 1977.

Azasu, Kwakuvi. "Beggars' Lore." Review of *The Beggars' Strike. Africa* 139 (March 1983): 63-64.

Bâ, Mariama. "La Fonction politique des littératures africaines écrites." *Ecriture française dans le monde* 5.1 (1981): 3-7.

Beauvoir, Simone de. "France: Feminism - Alive, Well and in Constant Danger." *Sisterhood Is Global.* Ed. Robin Morgan. Garden City, N.Y.: Anchor Press/Doubleday, 1984.

Bell, Roseann. "The Absence of the African Woman Writer." *C.L.A. Journal* 21 (1978): 491-98.

___. ed. *Sturdy Black Bridges: Visions of Black Women in Literature.* New York: Anchor, 1979.

Bennett, Pramila R. Review of. *A Dakar Childhood. Africa* 147 (November 1983): 71.

Benstock, Shari, ed. *Feminist Issues in Literary Scholarship.* Bloomington: Indiana University Press, 1987.

Berrian, Brenda. *Bibliography of African Women Writers and Journalists.* Washington, D. C.: Three Continents Press, 1985.

Blair, Dorothy S. *African Literature in French.* Cambridge: Cambridge University Press, 1976.

___. "Etat et statut de la critique française de la littérature négro-africaine d'expression française." *Oeuvres et Critiques* (Autumn 1979): 39-52.

___. *Senegalese Literature: A Critical Literature.* Boston: Twayne, 1984.

Bobia, Rosa and Cheryl Wall Staunton. "Aminata Sow Fall: Ses Livres et Son Nouveau Rôle." *Présence Francophone* 36 (1990): 133-136.

Boni-Sirera, Jacqueline. "Littérature et société. Etude critique de *La Grève des Bàttu* d'Aminata Sow Fall." *Revue de Littérature et d'Esthétique négro-africaines* 5 (1984): 59-89.

Borgomano, Madeleine. *Lectures de l'Appel des arènes d'Aminata Sow Fall.* Abidjan: Les Nouvelles Editions Africaines, 1984.

Brench, A. C. *The Novelists' Inheritance in French Africa*. Oxford: Oxford University Press, 1967.

Brooks, George E. "The Signares of Saint-Louis and Goree: Women Entrepreneurs in Eighteenth Century Senegal." *Women in Africa*. Ed. Nancy J. Hafkin and Edna G. Bay. Stanford: Stanford University Press, 1976.

Brown, Ella. "Reactions To Western Values as reflected in African Novels." *Phylon* 48.3 (Fall 1987): 216-228.

Brown, Lloyd. *Women Writers in Black Africa*. Westport, Connecticut: Greenwood Press, 1981.

Bruner, Charlotte H. Review of *A Dakar Childhood*. *World Literature Today* 57.2 (1983): 339.

___. "A Decade for Women Writers." *African Literature Studies: The Present State/L'Etat present*. Ed. Stephen Arnold. Washington, D.C.: Three Continents Press, 1985.

___. "First Novels of Girlhood." *C.L.A. Journal* 31.3 (March 1988): 324-338.

___. *Unwinding Threads: Writing by Women in Africa*. London: Heinemann, 1983.

___. "Women Writers and Women's Role in Contemporary Black Africa." Unpublished Paper.

Cailler, Bernadette. "L'Aventure ambiguë: Autobiographie ou histoire d'un peuple." *The French Review* 55.6 (May,1982): 742-51. *World Literature Written in English* 21.3 (1982): 538-40.

Cazenave, Odile. "Gender, Age and Reeducations: A changing Emphasis in Recent African Novels in French as exemplified in *L'Appel des Arènes* by Aminata Sow Fall." *Africa Today* 38.3 (1991): 54-62.

___. "La Situation de la femme ecrivain au Sénégal: De Mariama Bâ à Aminata Sow Fall." Unpublished paper.

Cham, Mbye Baboucar. "Contemporary Society and the Female Imagination: A study of the Novels of Mariama Bâ." *Women in African Literature Today*. Ed. Eldred Durosimi Jones. Trenton, New Jersey: Africa World Press, 1987

___. "The Female Condition in Africa: A Literary Exploration by Mariama Ba." *A Current Bibliography on African Affairs* 17.1 (1984-85): 29-51.

Charles, Eunice A. "A History of the Kingdom of Jolof (Senegal) 1800-1890." Diss. Boston, 1973.

Chemain-Degrange, Arlette. "Emancipation féminine et littérature négro-africaine." *Annales de l'Université de Brazzaville* 9 (1973): 3-22.

___. *Emancipation féminine et roman africain.* Dakar: Les Nouvelles Editions Africaines, 1980.

___. "L'Image de la "Mère dévorante" *L'Afrique Littéraire* 54-55 (1979-1980): 92-98.

___. "La Promotion féminine à travers les romans africains." *Actuel Développement* 1 (1974): 35-39.

Chevrier, Jacques. "Comment travaillent les ecrivains: Aminata Sow Fall." *Jeune Afrique* 124 (April 11, 1984): 66-67.

___. *Littérature nègre*. 2nd ed. Paris: Armand Colin, 1984.

Chinweizu, Onwuchekua Jemie and Ihechukwu Madubuike. *Towards the Decolonization of African Literature*. Washington D.C.: Howard University Press, 1983.

Chodorow, Nancy. *The Reproduction of Mothering*. Berkeley: University of California Press, 1978.

La Civilisation de la femme dans la tradition africaine. Meeting organized by La Société Africaine de Culture, Abidjan 3-8 July, 1972). Paris: Présence Africaine, 1975.

Colin, Roland. *Littérature africaine d'hier et de demain*. Paris: A.D.E.C., 1965.

Condé, Maryse. "Three Female Writers in Modern Africa: Flora Nwapa, Ama Ata Aidoo and Grace Ogot." Presence Africaine 82 (1972): 132-43.

Cooke, Joanne. Bunch-Weeks Charlotte, and Robin Morgan, eds. *The New Women: A Motive Anthology on Women's Liberation*. Indianapolis: The Bobbs-Merrill Co. Inc., 1970.

Cornevin, Robert. *Littératures d'Afrique noire de langue française*. Presses universitaires de France, 1976.

Crosta, Suzanne. "Les Structures spatiales dans *L'Appel des Arènes* d'Aminata Sow Fall." *Revue francophone de Louisiane* (Spring 1988): 58-65.

Crowder, Michael. *Senegal. A Study in French Assimilation Policy.* London: Oxford University Press, 1962.

Crowder, Michael, and Donal Cruise O'Brien. "French West Africa 1945-1960." *History of West Africa* vol 2. Ed. J. F. Ade Ajayi and Michael Crowder. 2nd ed. New York: Columbia University Press, 1976.

Cruise O'Brien, Donal. *The Mourides of Senegal.* Oxford: Oxford University Press, 1971.

___. *Saints and Politicians: Essays in the Organisation of a Senegalese Peasant Society.* Cambridge: Cambridge University Press, 1975.

Cruise O'Brien, Rita. *White Society in Black Africa: The French of Senegal.* Evanston: Northwestern University Press, 1972.

D'Almeida, Irene Assiba. "The Concept of Choice in Mariama Bâ's Fiction." *Ngambika: Studies of Women in African Fiction.* Ed. Carole Boyce Davies and Anne Adams Graves. Trenton, New Jersey: Africa World Press Inc., 1986.

___. *Francophone African Women Writers: Destroying the Emptiness of Silence.* Gainesville: University Press of Florida, 1994.

Davidson, Basil. *Africa: History of a Continent.* New York: Macmillan, 1966.

Davies, Carole Boyce, and Anne Adams Graves, eds. *Ngambika: Studies of Women in African Literature.* Trenton, New Jersey: Africa World Press Inc., 1986.

Deleuze, Gilles, and Félix Guattari. *Kafka: Pour une littérature mineure.* Paris: Les Editions de Minuit, 1975.

Deves, Madeleine. "Le Rôle de la femme dans la pratique du droit coutumier. Exemple du Sénégal." *La Civilisation de la femme dans la tradition africaine.* Paris: Présence Africaine, 1975. 313-26.

Dia, Alioune Touré. "Succès littéraire de Mariama Bâ pour son livre *Une Si Longue Lettre.*" *Amina* 84 (1979): 12-14.

Diarra, Fatoumata-Agnès. *Femmes africaines en devenir: les femmes Zarma du Niger.* Paris: Editions Anthropos, 1971.

Diop, Abdoulaye-Bara. *La Société wolof.* Paris: Karthala, 1981.

Diop, Delyna Hayward. Review of *La Grève des Bàttu. Ufahamu* 11.2 (1981-82): 179-81.

Dorsinville, Roger. "Vies d'Afrique: Une Collection Vérité." *Notre Librairie* 81 (1985): 147-50.

Doubrovsky, Serge. "Autobiographie/Vérité/Psychanalyse." *L'Esprit Créateur* 20.3 (Fall,1980): 87-97.

Dunton, Chris. Review of *Un Chant écarlate. West Africa* 3475 (26 March 1982): 725-26.

Edson, Laurie. "Mariama Bâ and the Politics of the Family." *Studies in Twentieth Century Literature* 17.1 (Winter 1993): 13-25.

Egon, Susanna. *Patterns of Experience in Autobiography.* Chapel Hill, North Carolina: University of North Carolina Press, 1984.

Egonu, I. T. K. "Aminata Sow Fall: A New Generation Female Writer from Senegal." *Neophilologus* (January 1991): 66-75.

Erickson, John D. *Nommo: African Fiction in French South of the Sahara.* York, South Carolina: French Literary Publications Co., 1979.

F.A. "Sénégal: Des récits à lire en se promenant." Review of *Gens de sable. Jeune Afrique* 1247 (28 November 1984): 67.

Faladé, Solange. "Femmes de Dakar et de son agglomération." *Femmes d'Afrique noire.* Ed. Denise Paulme. Paris: Mouton Et Co., 160. 207-16.

Fetzer, Glenn W. "Women's Search for Voice and the Problem of Knowing in the Novels of Mariama Bâ." *C.L.A. Journal* 35.1 (September 1991): 31-41.

Flannigan, Arthur. "African Discourse and the Autobiographical Novel: Mongo Beti's Mission Terminee." *The French Review* 55.6 (May 1982): 835-45.

Flewellen, Elinor. "Assertiveness versus Submissiveness in Selected Works by African Women Writers." *Ba Shiru* 12.2 (1985): 3-18.

Fougeyrollas, Pierre. *Modernisation des hommes.* Paris: Flammarion, 1967.

Frank, Katherine. "Feminist Criticism and the African Novel." *African Literature Today* 14 (1984): 34-38.

Gadjigo, Samba. "Social Vision in Aminata Sow Fall's Literary work." *World Literature Today* (Summer 1989): 411-15.

Gamble, Daryll Forde. *The Wolof of Senegambia*. London: International African Institute, 1957.

Gellar, Sheldon. *Senegal: An African Nation between Islam and the West*. Boulder, Colorado: Westview Press, 1982.

Gérard, Albert, and Jeannine Laurent. "Sembène's Progeny: A New Trend in the Senegalese Novel." *Studies in Twentieth Century Literature* 4.2 (1980): 133-45.

Gilligan, Carol. *In a Different Voice: Psychological Theory and Women's Development*. Cambridge, Massachusetts: Harvard University Press, 1982.

Gleason, Judith. *This Africa: Novels by West Africans in English and French*. Evanston: Northwestern University Press, 1965.

Guyonneau, Christine H. "Francophone Women Writers from Sub-Saharan Africa: A Preliminary Bibliography." *Callaloo* 8.2 (1985): 453-483

Hafkin, Nancy J., and Edna G. Bay, eds. *Women in Africa*. Stanford: Stanford University Press, 1976.

Hammond, Thomas. "Entretien avec Aminata Sow Fall." *Présence Francophone* 22 (1981): 191-95.

Harrell-Bond, Barbara. "Transcending Cultural Boundaries Through Fiction." *American Universities Field Staff Reports* 10 Africa (1982): 1-12.

___. "Interview avec Mariama Bâ le 9 juillet 1979." *African Book Publishing Record* 6 (1980): 209-14.

Harrow, Kenneth, ed. *Faces of Islam in African Literature*. Portsmouth, New Hampshire: Heinemann, 1991.

___. "The Poetics of African littérature de témoignage." *African Literature Studies: The Present State/L'Etat present*. Ed. Stephen Arnold. Washington, D.C.: Three Continents Press, 1985.

Hawkins, Peter. "An Interview with Senegalese Novelist Aminata Sow Fall." *French Studies Bulletin* (Spring 1987): 19-21.

Herzberger-Fofana, Pierrette. *Ecrivains africains et identités culturels - Entretiens*. Tübingen: Stauffenburg Verlag, 1989.

___. "L'Islam dans les romans féminins sénégalais." *Frankophone Literaturen Außerhalb Europas*. Ed. János Riesz. Frankfurt am Main: Peter Lang, 1987.

___. "La Littérature féminine francophone: Les romancières sénégalaises." *Französisch Heute* 4 (December 1985): 407-420.

Hurel, Lucie. Review of *La Parole aux Négresses*. *Peuples Noirs, Peuples Africains* 5 (Sept-Oct.1978): 5-69.

Irele, Abiola. Review of *Une Si Longue Lettre*. *African Book Publishing Records* 6.2 (1980): 108-09.

Izevbaye, Dan. "Issues in the Reassessment of the African Novel." *African Literature Today* 10 (1979): 8-27.

Jaccard, Amy Claire. "Les Visages de l'Islam chez Mariama Bâ et chez Aminata Sow Fall." *Nouvelles du Sud* 6 (1986-1987): 171-182.

Jacobus, Mary. *Reading Women: Essays in Feminist Criticism.* New York: Columbia University Press, 1986.

James, Adeola. *In Their Own Voices: African Women Writers Talk.* London: James Currey, 1990.

Jiagge, Annie. "Looking Towards the Future: The Role of Women in Africa's Evolution." *La Civilisation de la femme dans la tradition africaine.* Paris: Presence Africaine, 1975.

Jones, Eldred Durosimi, ed. *Women in African Literature Today.* Trenton, New Jersey: Africa World Press, 1987.

Joppa, Francis Anani. *L'Engagement des ecrivains africains noirs de langue française.* Sherbrooke: Naaman, 1982.

Ka, Aminata Maïga. "Ramatoulaye, Aïssatou, Mireille et ... Mariama Bâ." *Notre Librairie* 81 (Oct-Dec. 1981): 129-34.

Ka, Omar. "Une Nouvelle Place pour le français au Sénégal." *The French Review* 67.2 (December 1993): 276-290.

Kamara, Sylviane. "Une Sénégalaise prix Goncourt." *Jeune Afrique* (1 August 1979): 64.

Kane, Mohamadou. "The African Writer and His Public." *African Writers on African Writing.* Ed. G. D. Killam. Evanston: Northwestern University Press, 1973: 53-68.

___. *Roman africain et traditions.* Dakar: Les Nouvelles Editions Africaines, 1982.

___. "Structures: Sur 'les Formes traditionnelles' du roman africain." *Revue de Littérature comparée* 3-4 (1974): 536-68.

Kayo, Patrick. "Le Dilemme de l'ecrivain en Afrique aujourd'hui." *Présence Africaine* 103 (1977): 126-28.

Kesteloot, Lilyan, ed. *Anthologie Négro-Africaine*. Verviers: Marabout Université, 1976.

___. *Les Ecrivains noirs de Langue française*. Brussels: Editions de L'Université de Bruxelles, 1963.

Kembe, Milolo. *L'Image de la femme chez les romancières de l'Afrique noire francophone*. Fribourg, Switzerland: Editions Universitaires, 1986.

Kemp, Yakini. "Romantic Love and the Individual in Novels by Mariama Bâ, Buchi Emecheta, and Bessie Head." *Obsidian II* 3.3 (Winter 1988): 1-16.

Killam, G. D., ed. *African Writers on African Writing*. Evanston: Northwestern University, 1973.

Kilson, Marion. "Women in African Literature." *Journal of African Studies* 4.2 (1977): 161-66.

Kom, Ambroise, ed. *Dictionnaire des Oeuvres littéraires négro-africaines de Langue francaise*. Sherbrooke: Naaman, 1983.

Kuoh-Moukoury, Thérèse. *Les Couples Dominos*. Paris: Juillard, 1973.

Lambrech, Regina. "Three Black Women, Three Autobiographers." *Presence Africaine* 123 (3e trim. 1982): 136-43.

Langlois, Emile. "De Tilène au Plateau: Review." *Dictionnaire des oeuvres littéraires négro-africaines de langue française.* Ed. Ambroise Kom. Sherbrooke: Naaman, 1983. 168-69.

Larrier, Renée. "Correspondance et Création littéraire: Mariama Bâ's *Une Si Longue Lettre.*" *The French Review* 64.5 (April 1991): 747-753.

Larson, Charles R. *The Emergence of African Fiction.* 2nd ed. Bloomington: Indiana University Press, 1972.

Laye, Camara. "The Soul of Africa in Guinea." *African Literature and the Universities.* Ed. Gerald Moore. Ibadan: Ibadan University Press, 1965.

Lee, Sonia. "The Awakening of the Self in the Heroines of Ousmane Sembène." *Sturdy Black Bridges: Visions of Black Women in Literature.* Ed. Roseann Bell. New York: Anchor, 1979.

___. "L'image de la femme dans le roman francophone de l'Afrique Occidentale." Diss. Massachusetts, 1974.

___. "Le Thème du bonheur chez les romancières de l'Afrique occidentale." *Présence Francophone* 29 (1986): 91-103.

Lejeune, Philippe. *Le Pacte autobiographique.* Paris: Editions du Seuil, 1975.

Lemotieu, Martin. "L'Interférence de la religion musulmane sur les Structures actuelles de la société négro-africaine: L'Exemple de *La Grève des Bàttu* d'Aminata Sow Fall." *Nouvelles du Sud* 6 (1986-87): 49-60.

Lindfors, Bernth. "Politics, Culture and Literary Form in Black Africa." *Colby Literary Quarterly* 15 (1979): 240-251

Linton-Umeh, Marie. "The African Heroine." *Sturdy Black Bridges: Visions of Black Women in Literature.* Ed. Roseann Bell. New York: Anchor, 1979.

Little, Kenneth. *The Sociology of Urban Women's Image in African Literature.* Totowa, New Jersey: Macmillan, 1980.

Luce, Louise Fiber. "Passages: the Women of sony Labou Tansi." *The French Review* 64.5 (April 1991): 739-746.

Lunel, Armand. *Sénégal.* Lausanne: Editions Rencontre, 1966.

Madubuike, Ihechukwu. *The Senegalese Novel: A Sociological Study of the Impact of the Politics of Assimilation.* Washington, D.C.: Three Continents Press, 1983.

Magnier, Bernard. "Ken Bugul ou l'Ecriture thérapeutique." *Notre Librairie* 81 (Oct.-Dec. 1985): 151-55.

Makward, Christiane with Odile Cazenave. "The Others' Others: 'Francophone' Women and Writing." *Yale French Studies* 75, Fall 1988:190-207.

Makward, Edris. "Marriage, Tradition and Woman's Pursuit of Happiness in the Novels of Mariama Bâ." *Ngambika: Studies of Women in African Literature.* Eds. Carol Boyce Davies and Anne Adams Graves. Trenton, New Jersey: Africa World Press Inc., 1986.

Marks, Elaine, and Isabelle De Courtivron, eds. *New French Feminisms.* Amherst: University of Massachusetts Press, 1980.

Martin, Victor and Charles Becker. "Les *Teen* du Baol: Essai de Chronologie." *Bulletin de L'I.F.A.N.* Dakar 38.B.3 (1976): 449-505.

May, Georges. *L'Autobiographie.* Paris: Presses Universitaires de France, 1979.

Mbacké, Mame Seck. "Littérature africaine et littérature latino-américaine." *Ethiopiques* 1.3 (1983): 201-205.

Mbaye, Annette. "Une Victoire des Sénégalaises." *Jeune Afrique* 367 (1968): 34-35.

Mbiti, John S. *African Religions and Philosophy.* New York: Frederick A. Praeger, 1969.

McCaffrey, Kathleen M. "Images of Women in West African Literature and Film: A Struggle Against Dual Colonization." *International Journal of Women's Studies* 3.1 (Jan/Feb, 1980): 76-88.

McConnell-Ginet, Sally, Ruth Borker, and Nelly Furman, eds. *Women and Language in Literature and Society.* New York: Praeger Publishers, 1980.

McCullough, Richard Cysle. "The Novels of Camara Laye: A Study of Selected Themes." Diss. University of Colorado, 1980.

McElaney-Johnson, Ann. "The Place of the Woman or the Woman Displaced in Mariama Bâ's *Une Si Longue Lettre. C.L.A. Journal* 37.1 (September 1993): 19-28.

Meese, Elizabeth A. *Crossing the Double-Cross: The Practice of Feminist Criticism.* Chapel Hill: The University of North Carolina Press, 1986.

Mérand, Patrick. *La Vie quotidienne en Afrique noire à travers la littérature africaine.* Paris: L'Harmattan, 1980.

Mérand, Patrick, and Sewanou Dabla. *Guide de littérature africaine de langue française.* Paris: L'Harmattan, 1979.

Michelman, Frederic. Review of *L'Appel des Arènes. World Literature Today* 58.1 (1984): 153-54.

___. "The West African Novel Since 1911." *Yale French Studies* 53 (1976): 29-44

Miller, Christopher L. *Theories of Africans: Francophone Literature and Anthropology in Africa.* Chicago: University of Chicago Press, 1990.

Miller, Elinor S. "Contemporary Satire in Senegal: Aminata Sow Fall's *La Grève des Bàttu." French Literature Series* 14 (1987): 143-151.

___. "Two Faces of the Exotic: Mariama Bâ's *Un Chant écarlate." French Literature Series* 13 (1986): 144-147.

Millstone, Amy B. Review of *Un Chant écarlate. African Book Publishing Record* 10.3 (1984): 154.

Mokwenye, Cyril. "Aminata Sow Fall as Social Critic: An Interpretation of *Le Revenant* and *La Grève des Bàttu." Neohelicon* 19.2 (1992): 211-21.

___. "La Polygamie et la révolte de la femme africaine moderne: Une Lecture d'*Une Si Longue Lettre* de Mariama Ba." *L'Afrique Littéraire* 63-66 (1982): 59-64.

Monteil, Vincent. "Lat-Dyor, Damel of Kayor (1842-86) and the Islamization of the Wolof of Senegal." *Islam in Tropical Africa*. Ed. I. M. Lewis. Bloomington, Indiana: International African Institute, 1980.

___. "The Wolof Kingdom of Kayor." *West African Kingdoms in the Nineteenth Century*. Ed. Daryll Forde and P. M. Kaberry. London: Oxford University Press, 1967.

Moore, Carrie Dailey. "Evolution of an African Artist: Social Realism in the Works of Sembène Ousmane." Diss. Indiana, 1973.

Moore, Gerald, ed. *African Literature and the Universities*. Ibadan: Ibadan University Press, 1965.

Morgan, Robin, ed. *Sisterhood Is Global*. Garden City, New York: Anchor Press/Doubleday, 1984.

Mortimer, Mildred. "Enclosure/Disclosure in Mariama Bâ's *Une Si Longue Lettre*." *The French Review* 64.1 (October 1990): 69-78.

___. "Espace féminin." Unpublished Paper.

___. *Journeys through the French African Novel*. Portsmouth, New Hampshire: Heinemann, 1990.

Moumouni, Abdou. *Education en Afrique* 1964. *Education in Africa* translated by Phyllis Nauts Ott. London: André Deutsch, 1968.

Mouralis, Bernard. *Littérature et Développement*. Editions Silex/Agence de Coopération Culturelle et technique, 1984.

Mudimbe-Boyi, Elizabeth. "The Poetics of Exile and Errancy in *Le Baobab fou* by Ken Bugul and *Ti Jean L'Horizon* by Simone Schwarz-Bart." *Yale French Studies* 2.83 (1993): 196-212.

___. "Les voix multiples in Bâ's *Une Si Longue Lettre*." Unpublished paper

Mutiso, G.-C. M. *Socio-Political Thought in African Literature*. London: Macmillan, 1974.

Nalova Lyonga, Pauline. "Uhamiri Or a Feminist Approach to African Literature: An Analysis of Selected Texts by Women in Oral and Written Literature." Diss. Michigan, 1985.

N'Diaye, Catherine. "La Passion de la Langue." *La Quinzaine Littéraire* 436 (March 1985): 16.

Ndongko, Theresa. "Tradition and the Role of Women in Africa." *Presence Africaine* 99-100 (1976): 143-154

Ngandu, Pius Nkashama. *Littératures africaines de 1930 à nos jours*. Paris: Silex, 1984.

Ngate, Jonathan. *Francophone African Fiction: Reading a Literary Tradition*. Trenton, New Jersey: Africa World Press, 1988.

Ngcobo, Lauretta. "Four Women Writers in Africa Today." *South African Outlook* (May 1984): 64-69.

Niang, Sada. "Modes de Contextualisations dans *Une Si Longue Lettre* et *L'Appel des arènes*." *The Literary Griot* 4.1-2 (Spring-Fall 1992): 111-125.

Nwachukwo-Agbada, J. O. J. "'One Wife be for one Man': Mariama Bâ's Doctrine for Matrimony." *Modern Fiction Studies* 37.3 (1991): 561-573.

Obiechina, Emmanuel. *Culture, Tradition and Society in the West African Novel.* Cambridge: Cambridge University Press, 1975.

Ogundipe-Leslie, Molara. "The Female Writer and her Commitment." *Women in African Literature Today.* Ed. Eldred D. Jones. Trenton, New Jersey: Africa World Press, 1987.

Ojo-Ade, Femi. "Female Writers, Male Critics." *African Literature Today* 13 (1982): 158-78.

___. "Still a Victim? Mariama Ba's Une Si Longue Lettre." *African Literature Today* 12 (1982): 71-87.

Okafor, Nididi R. "Aminata Sow Fall: Cas du *Revenant. Neohelicon* 18.1 (1991): 89-97.

Okeke-Ezigbo, Emeka. "Begging the Beggars: Restoration of the Dignity of Man in *The Beggars' Strike. Neohelicon* 19.1 (1992):307-22.

Olney, James. *Tell Me Africa: An Approach to African Literature.* Princeton: Princeton University Press, 1973.

Oloruntimehin B.Olatunji. "The Western Sudan and the Coming of the French 1800-1893." *History of West Africa.* 2nd ed. Vol 2. Eds. J.F. Ade Ajayi and Michael Crowder. New York: Columbia University Press, 1976.

Ortova, Jarmila. "Les Femmes dans l'oeuvre littéraire d'Ousmane Sembène." *Présence Africaine* 70 (1969): 69-77.

O'Toole, Thomas. Review of *Le Froid et le piment.* *African Book Publishing Record* 10.4 (1984): 227-28.

Pageard, Robert. *Littérature négro-africaine.* Paris: Le Livre africain, 1966.

Pala, Achola O. "Definitions of Women and Development: An African Perspective." *Women and National Development.* Ed. B. Ximena Bunster et al. Chicago: University of Chicago Press, 1977.

Palmer, Eustace. *The Growth of the African Novel.* London: Heinemann, 1979.

___. *An Introduction to the African Novel.* New York: Africana Publishing Corporation, 1972.

Paulme, Denise, ed. *Femmes d'Afrique noire.* Paris: Mouton et Co., 1960.

Perry, Ruth. *Women, Letters and the Novel.* New York: Ams Press, 1980.

Pfaff, Francoise. "Aminata Sow Fall: L'Ecriture au féminin." *Notre Librairie* 81 (1985): 135-38.

___. "Enchantment and Magic in Two Novels by Aminata Sow Fall." *C. L. A. Journal* 31.3 (March 1988): 339-359.

Pieterse, Cosmo, and Dennis Duerden, eds. *African Writers Talking*. New York: Africana Publishing Corporation, 1972.

Pieterse, Cosmo, and Donald Munro, eds. *Protest and Conflict in African Literature*. London: Heinemann, 1969.

Porter, Laurence M. "Senegalese Literature Today." *The French Review* 66.6 (May 1993): 887-899.

Radio broadcast of interviews with Aminata Ka, Aminata Sow Fall, and Mame Seck Mbacke at the Dakar Book Fair. "L'Ecriture féminine au Sénégal", Antipodes. France Culture. 1986.

Rauf, Muhammad Abdul. *Islam: Creed and Worship*. Washington, D.C.: The Islamic Center, 1974.

Riesz, János. "Mariama Bâ's *Une Si Longue Lettre*: An Erziehungsroman." Translated by Richard Bjornson. *Research in African Literatures* 22.1 (Spring 1991): 27-42.

Robertson, Claire and Iris Berger. *Women and Class in Africa*. New York: Africana Publishing Co., 1986.

Rushing, Andrea B. "Images of Black Women in Modern African Poetry: An Overview." *Sturdy Black Bridges: Visions of Black Women in Literature*. Ed. Roseann Bell. New York: Anchor, 1979.

Sahel, André-Patrick. "L'Afrique aux Africaines." *Actuel Développement* 40 (1981): 39-40.

___. "Une Tragédie de la dissémination: *Le Fort maudit* de Nafissatou Diallo." *Afrique Littéraire* 63-64 (1982): 83-84.

Sarvan, Charles Ponnuthurai. "Feminism and African Fiction: the Novels of Mariama Bâ." *Modern Fiction Studies* 34.3 (Autumn 1988): 453-464.

Savane, Marie-Angélique. "Senegal: Elegance Amid the Phallocracy." *Sisterhood Is Global.* Ed. Robin Morgan. Garden City, New York: Anchor Press/Doubleday, 1984.

Schipper, Mineke., ed. *Unheard Words: Women and Literature in Africa, the Arab World, Asia, the Caribbean, and Latin America.* Translated by Barbara Potter Fasting. London: Allison and Busby, 1985.

Senghor, Leopold. "Constructive Elements of a Civilization of African Negro Inspiration." *Présence Africaine* 24-25 (1959): 262-94.

Senghor, Rose, and Aminata Sow. "Le Rôle d'educatrice de la femme africaine dans la civilisation traditionnelle." *La Civilisation de la femme dans la tradition africaine.* Paris: Présence Africaine, 1975. 232-41.

Slomski, Genevieve T. "Dialogue in the Discourse: A Study of Revolt in Selected Fiction by African Women." Diss. Indiana U., 1985.

Smith, Esther. Review of *Collier de Cheville. African Book Publishing Record* 10.1 (1984): 29.

Smith, Robert P. "Portrayal of Interracial Couples in the Black Novel of French Expression." C.L.A. Journal 22 (1978): 14-23.

Sow Fall, Aminata. "Du pilon à la machine à écrire." *Notre Librairie* 68 (1983): 73-77.

___. "Pratiques langagières dans la littérature négro-africaine de langue française." *Ethiopiques* 3, 1-2 (1985): 61-66.

Sow, Fatou. "Femmes, socialité et valeurs africaines." *Notes Africaines* 168 (1980): 105-12.

___. "Muslim Families in Contemporary Black Africa." *Current Anthropology* 26.5 (1885): 563-70.

Soyinka, Wole. *Myth, Literature and the African World*. Cambridge: Cambridge University Press, 1976.

Ssensalo, Bede M. "The Black Pseudo-Autobiographical Novel: Miss Jane Pittman and Houseboy." *African Literature Today* 14 (1984): 93-109.

Staunton, Cheryl Wall. "Mariama Bâ: Pioneer Senegalese Woman Novelist." *C. L. A. Journal* 37.3 (March 1994): 328-335.

Steady, Filomina C. *The Black Woman Cross-Culturally*. Cambridge, Massachusetts: Schenkman Publishing Co. Inc., 1981.

Stegeman, Beatrice. "The Divorce Dilemma: The New Woman in Contemporary African Novels." *Critique: Studies in Modern Fiction* 15.3 (1974): 81-92.

Stratton, Florence. "The Shallow Grave: Archetypes of Female Experience in African Fiction." *Research in African Literatures* 19.1 (Summer 1988): 143-169.

Stringer, Susan. "Cultural Conflict in the Novels of Two African Writers, Mariama Bâ and Aminata Sow Fall." *Sage: A Scholarly Journal on Black Women.* Student Supplement 1988: 36-40.

___. "Innovation in Ken Bugul's *Le Baobab fou.*" *Cincinnati Romance Review* X (1991): 200-207.

___. "Nafissatou Diallo: A Pioneer in Black African Writing." *Continental, Latin American and Francophone Women Writers Volume II.* Eds. Ginette Adamson and Eunice Myers. Lanham, Maryland: University Press of America, 1990

Taiwo, Oladele. *Female Novelists of Modern Africa.* New York: St. Martin's Press, 1984.

Thiam, Awa. *La Parole aux Négresses.* Editions Denoël/ Gonthier, 1978.

Thioune, Babacar. Review of *Un Chant écarlate. Notre Librairie* 68 (Jan-Apr. 1983): 89-90.

Trimingham, John Spencer. *A History of Islam in West Africa.* London: Oxford University Press, 1962.

Trinh, T. Minh-ha. "Aminata Sow Fall et l'espace du don." *The French Review* 55.6 (1982): 780-89.

Turnbull, Colin M. *The Lonely African.* New York: Simon and Schuster, 1962.

Van Allen, Judith. "Women in Africa. Modernization Means More Dependancy." *The Center Magazine* 7.3 (1974): 60-67.

Volet, Jean-Marie. "Romancières francophones d'Afrique Noire: Vingt Ans d'activités littéraires à découvrir." *The French Review* 65.5 (April 1992): 765-773.

Wachtel, Eleanor. "The Mother and the Whore." *Umoja* 2 (1977): 31-48.

Wake, Clive. "The Political and Cultural Revolution." *Protest and Conflict in African Literature.* Ed. Cosmo Pieterse and Donald Munro. London: Heinemann, 1969.

Wallace, Karen Smyley. "Women and Identity: A Black Francophone Female Perspective." *Sage* 11.1 (Spring 1985): 19-23.

Yewah, Emmanuel. "Sony Labou Tansi and His Unstable Political Figures." *The French Review* 67.1 (October 1993): 93-104.

Zell, Hans. "Report of First Noma Award for Publishing in Africa." *African Book Publishing Record* 6.3-4 (1980): 199.

Index

FRANCOPHONE CULTURES & LITERATURES

General Editors: Michael G. Paulson & Tamara Alvarez-Detrell

This series will include studies about the literature, culture, and civilization of all French-speaking countries except France, i.e. studies on the Francophone areas in Africa, the French-speaking islands in the Caribbean, as well as studies that deal with the French aspects in Canada. Cross-cultural studies between these geographic areas are also encouraged. The book-length manuscripts may be written in either English or French.

Authors wishing to have works considered for this series should send a one page synopsis to:

Dr. Michael G. Paulson
Department of Foreign Languages
Kutztown University
Kutztown, PA 19530